THE WORLD OF FOREVER

A MEMORIAL ANTHOLOGY OF QUOTATIONS
FROM THE MINACK CHRONICLES

Derek Tangye

Line drawings by Jean Nichol Tangye

CHIVERS LARGE PRINT
BATH

| British Library Cataloguing in Publication Data available |

This Large Print edition published by Chivers Press, Bath, 1998.

Published by arrangement with Hamish Hamilton Ltd.

U.K. Hardcover ISBN 0 7540 3413 5
U.K. Softcover   ISBN 0 7540 3414 3

Printed and bound in Great Britain by
Redwood Books, Trowbridge, Wiltshire

HEREFORDSHIRE
COUNCIL

Please return/renew this item by the
last date shown
Herefordshire Libraries and
Information Service

CONTENTS

Out of the stillness of the night I heard
Jeannie's voice:

> The Spirits of Minack
> Welcome you
> To their
> World of Forever
> Where life continues
> And death is never.

The Confusion Room

'THERE IT IS!'

The path we walked along was only a shadow of a path, more like the trodden run of badgers. Here, because there was no sign of habitation, because the land and the boulders and the rocks embraced the sea without interference, we could sense we were part of the beginning of time, the centuries of unceasing waves, the unseen pattern of the wild generations of foxes and badgers, the ageless gales that had lashed the desolate land, exultant and roaring, a giant harbour of sunken ships in their wake. And we came to a point, after a steep climb, where a great Carn stood balanced on a smaller one, upright like a huge man standing on a stool, as if it were a sentinel waiting to hail the ghosts of lost sailors. The track, on the other side, had tired of the undergrowth which blocked its way along the head of the cliff, for it sheered seawards tumbling in a zigzag course to the scarred grey rocks below. We stood on the pinnacle . . . the curve of Mount's Bay leading to the Lizard Point on the left, the Wolf Rock lighthouse a speck in the distance, a French crabber a mile offshore, pale blue hull and small green sail aft, chugging through the white speckled sea towards Newlyn, and high above us a buzzard, its wings spread motionless, soaring effortlessly into the sky.

Jeannie suddenly pointed inland. 'Look!' she said, 'there it is!'

3

There was never any doubt in either of our minds. The small grey cottage a mile away, squat in the lonely landscape, surrounded by trees and edged into the side of a hill, became as if by magic the present and the future. It was as if a magician beside this ancient Carn had cast a spell upon us, so that we could touch the future as we could, at that moment, touch the Carn. There in the distance we could see our figures moving about our daily tasks, a thousand, thousand figures criss-crossing the untamed land, dissolving into each other, leaving a mist of excitement of our times to come.

A Gull on the Roof

I still marvel at the luck that brought Jeannie and me to Minack. There are legions of people who yearn to pack up their jobs, and find some patch of land where they can create their earthly Nirvana. Jeannie and I were among that number who have succeeded in turning that dream into reality, but this was not achieved simply by exercising cold reason. We needed many unexpected circumstances to be on our side.

We both, for instance, had to share the wish to leave London, for failure would have been certain had one been dragging the other; and

4

it would have been understandable if Jeannie had hesitated about leaving the fun she had as publicity head of the Savoy, Claridge's and Berkeley. There were, too, the circumstances surrounding the discovery of Minack. The name, Lamorna, captured my imagination when I was a boy, but I never paid a visit to this lovely valley until one day in London I had a sudden urge to spend a few days' holiday there. Thus it was that Jeannie and I took a walk along the track above the harbour, then through chest-high bracken above the rocks and the sea until we climbed up the cliff to the point called Carn Barges. It was then that we saw the grey cottage inland, half hidden on the edge of a wood; and we knew from that instant we were going to live there.

Cottage on a Cliff

We had changed since we had first known each other, Jeannie and I. Once we had both fought hard to savour flattery and power, to be part of a glad world of revelry, to be in the fashion, and to rush every day at such speed that we disallowed ourselves any opportunity to ponder where we were going ... It is easy to remain in a groove, a groove which becomes worn without you realising it, only recognisable by friends who have not seen you for a long time, and it is usually luck which enables you to escape. Jeannie and I had the luck to feel the same at the same time, and so we had been united in forcing ourselves to flee our conventional background.

A Donkey in the Meadow

My life, after victory came, was not as straightforward as Jeannie's. I suddenly woke up to realise that I had passed the age of irresponsible dreams. And yet the dreams persisted, making me puzzled and restless and unsure. It was as if I were meeting myself again after five years wearing the same clothes ... there was the old self, however much I might have appeared to have changed in the meantime. I still wanted to play a lone role. I still knew that my mind would curdle if I were subject to an authority which I despised. These were the feelings I had always had; and they were supported by the knowledge that Jeannie felt as I did. We both believed that independence rather than conventional success was the greatest prize to possess.

But such an attitude has to measure up to reality. We were like countless others who, wanting to be free, had not the means which could provide such freedom. We could only muddle our way to the goal we were aiming at, hoping that fate would lead us there. We were not yet ready to do anything drastic. We were content to wait . . .

The Way to Minack

Jeannie loved her job. She was, however, a wise person. She had as much fun as anyone could wish for, but the pleasure from it was tempered slowly but surely by the realization that the same kind of fun was being endlessly repeated; and that one day she would weary of it. Moreover in war time there was a purpose to her work, worthwhile achievements were to be gained by her efforts; but in peace time she was often made use of by those with trivial intentions. Some would try to lure her co-operation in a publicity stunt, others would earnestly ask her help, only to forget her once she had given it. She gradually became distrustful of people; and yet, and this was the charm of her, she was always ready to trust again.

The Way to Minack

It was no ordinary cliff. It did not fall fearsomely sheer to the sea below but dropped, a jungle of thorns, gorse, elderberry trees and waist high couch grass, in a series of leaps to a rugged teaspoon of a bay; and as we stood there, somnolent gulls sitting on the

7

rocks far below, we saw in our minds a giant knife slicing pocket meadows out of the rampaging vegetation, refashioning the cliff so that it resembled the neat pattern of daffodil and potato gardens that were grouped like hillside Italian vineyards at intervals along the coast. We saw in our minds not only a way of life, but also the means by which to earn a living. It was the sweet moment when the wings of enthusiasm take flight, when victory is untarnished by endeavour, the intoxicating instant when the urge for conquest obliterates the reality of obstacles, dissolving common sense, blanketing the possibilities of failure. We had found our imaginary home.

A Gull on the Roof

'Absolute nonsense!' said the Chairman when she saw him, 'you're obviously tired and want a rest. Take six months holiday with pay' ... then added: 'When you come back you will want to stay with us for ever.'

I could understand his scepticism for he had no knowledge of the months of reasoning which had brought us to this moment. He could only comprehend the fact she was throwing away a career of distinction in favour of a wild adventure which, after a short while, might appear as a misplaced enthusiasm.

He could not be expected to appreciate the

sense of futility which perforce invades the kind of life we had been leading. The glamour and hospitality act as a narcotic, doping the finer instincts of living, and in the grey hours of early morning you lie awake painfully aware that you live in a flashy world where truth and integrity for the most part are despised, where slickness reigns supreme.

We Found the pace too fast and any material rewards poor substitutes for the peace of mind which was sacrificed. The world of politics, journalism and entertainment in which we moved requires a ruthless zest for professional survival if you are to do so, and this neither of us now possessed. It is a world in which you cannot live on prestige alone for it is only the present that counts. We had come to distrust both the importance of the objectives and the methods used to achieve them; for it is a world in which acclaim, however transitory and gained at whatever moral cost, is valued in the same currency as the conquest of Everest.

The atmosphere corrodes the individual and it had been corroding Jeannie and me. The moment of self-criticism, the shame we felt for our arid minds, slipped into oblivion as soon as we were in the splash of another party, in a cuckoo land of mutual admiration and sudden rip-roaring friendships.

There was no decisive occasion when we decided to leave. It was a host of occasions mingled into one, so that one day we suddenly realized our life was a spinning top, dizzily circling on one spot. We saw our fate, if we remained, in the men and women around us who had taken no heed of the barrier between youth and middle age, braying prejudiced views, dependent on values that toppled upside down, propping against a future which repeats endlessly the present, resembling worn playing cards. We could either drift on, or start again. We could either suffer the illusion our life was a contented one, remain within the environment we knew too well, or seek a freedom in a strange one.

A Gull on the Roof

It was nearly midnight, on that first visit, when the three of us reached Penzance. A gale was blowing in from the sea and as we drove along the front cascades of spray drenched the car as if coming from a giant hose. We crossed Newlyn Bridge, then up steep Paul Hill and along the winding road past the turn to Lamorna Valley; then up another hill, Boleigh Hill, where King Athelstan fought the Cornish ten centuries ago. Rain was whipping the windscreen when we turned off the road along a lane, through the dark shadows of a farm, until it petered out close to the cliff's edge. I got out and opened a gate, then drove bumpily across a field with the headlights swathing a way through a carpet of escaping rabbits. This, the back entrance to Minack, was the way we had to use until the bramble covered lane was opened up again; and after I pulled up beside a stone hedge, we still had two fields to scramble across in the darkness and the rain and the gale before we reached the cottage.

I lit a candle and the light quivered on the peeling, yellow papered walls. Everything was the same as the day we first pushed open the door; the ancient Cornish range, the pint sized rooms with their matchbox thick divisions, the wooden floor peppered with holes—only it was raining now and above the howl of the gale was the steady drip, drip of water from the leaking roof.

11

We didn't care. The adventure had begun.

A Gull on the Roof

HERE WAS TRANQUILLITY

We awoke the following morning to the sun streaming through the curtainless windows, to the distant murmur of the sea, to a robin's song hailing another day, and the delicious sensation that there was no frontier to our future. If our watches stopped what did it matter? An hour, a day, a week could pass . . . there was no barrier to which we were advancing, no date on a calendar which glared at us from a distance. No telephone to shiver us into expectation. No early morning noises, a far off factory hooter, the first rumble of traffic, the relentless roar of a Tube . . . no man-made alarms to jerk us into the beginning of another day. No newspaper shoved under the door. No clatter of milk bottles. Time to think, time to read. Go down to the rocks and stare vacantly at the sea. Perform insignificant, slowly achieved tasks—weeding the garden, mending a bolt on the door, sticking photographs in an album—without conscience nagging us with guilt. Take idle walks, observe the flight of a raven, the shifting currents of the sea, the delicate shades of moss. Travel the hours on horseback. Timelessness, isolation and simplicity creating the space which would protect us from the past. The hazy happiness of the present guiding our future.

A Gull on the Roof

We never had to wake up in the morning and say to each other that we wished to be somewhere else. We never had to daydream about the perfect home. We were in it.

A Drake at the Door

But the wonder of our life was that we never wished to shift its base. There in the lonely cottage where the sea murmured through the windows, we had the exquisite knowledge that if the map of the world had been open to us and we could go where we chose, money no object, we would have lived nowhere else. We were the lucky ones. We had an environment which cushioned us against the worries which burrow and sap confidence. We were living the life of our choice and Minack was our armour. We were not looking out at the horizon like others, searching for a life that is beyond reach. We did not have to say we would find happiness if we did this or did that, having to brighten the greyness of the passing years by praying that one day a dream would be fulfilled. We had our dream around us; and if there were times when the conventional stresses of living jabbed at us, challenging the sincerity of our happiness, we could not for long remain depressed. For we only had the trouble in hand to face.

A Drake at the Door

In this impermanent world in which restlessness is a deception for contentment, in which the individual can only salvage what he can from the twilight pressures of the mass, in which to be sensitive is no longer a grace, in which haste without purpose, second-hand pleasures, package thinking and noise for the sake of it are the gods of millions; in which truth is an expendable virtue in the pursuit of power, and in which youth is compelled from the beginning to worship materialism, Jeannie and I could touch the old stones of Minack, brace ourselves before the gales, listen to the sea talking and to the gulls crying, be at one with the animals, have time to search our inward selves and fight the shadow which is the enemy; and to marvel at the magic which had led us to a life we loved so much.

A Donkey in the Meadow

It is no ordinary coast. The stretch where Minack lies and where Jane's cottage still stands gaunt, staring out at the ocean, is not the kind of country which appeals to the conformist. The splendour of the cliffs does not lead to beaches where people can crowd together, transistors beside them.

The cliffs fall to rocks black and grey where the sea ceaselessly churns, splashing its foam, clutching a rock then releasing it, smothering it suddenly in bad temper, caressing it, slapping it as if in play, sometimes kind with the sun shining on the white ribbon of a wave, a laughing sea throwing spray like confetti, sometimes grey and sullen, then suddenly again a sea of ungovernable fury lashing the cliffs; enraged that for ever and for ever the cliffs look down.

And among the rocks are the pools; some that tempt yet are vicious, beckoning innocently then in a flash a cauldron of currents, pools that are shallow so that the minnow fish ripple the surface as they dash from view, pools so deep that seaweed looks like a forest far below, inaccessible pools, pools which hide from everyone except those who belong to them.

High above, the little meadows dodge the boulders, and where the land is too rough for cultivation the bracken, the hawthorn, the brambles, the gorse which sparks its yellow the year round, reign supreme. This is no place for interlopers. The walkers, tamed by pavements, faced by the struggling undergrowth, turn back or become angry, their standardised minds piqued that they have to race a way through; and it is left to the few, the odd man or

18

woman, to marvel that there is a corner of England still free from the dead hand of the busybody.

A Drake at the Door

Every day of our lives was spent in unison with this coast, the rage of the gales, salt smearing our faces as we walked, east winds, south winds, calm summer early mornings, the first cubs, a badger in the moonlight, wild violets, the glory of the first daffodil, the blustering madness of making a living on land that faced the roar of the ages. These were the passages of our year. Glorious, hurting, awakening us to the splendour of living. But the philistines. They nose. They want to disturb. Yet they are blind to beauty. They glance at our coast as they rush by. They want to see a path on the map. That is their object. Everything must conform. No time to pause. Hurry, hurry, hurry . . . we have another two miles to go.

A Drake at the Door

As the years went by our minds became more and more involved in the mystique of the Minack cliff. We would walk away from the cottage, isolated as it was from the fractious activity and noise of modern civilisation, yet arrive at the cliff meadows and find ourselves in another world. It was as if a spiritual cloak, born at the beginning of time, enveloped us. Here was tranquillity. No artificial stresses to upset it. No human being watching. No evil actions to threaten us. Nature was in charge.

The Confusion Room

We sat on the rickety seat in the Honeysuckle Meadow, Ambrose between us. We had strolled there before breakfast, the early morning sun warming us, and touching the honeysuckle, strengthening its scent. The meadow has an earth-filled stone hedge on one side, and it is guarded on the other side by a low, drystone wall. Around the rickety seat was a canopy of green leaves from an elder tree; and bushing along the drystone wall, facing the rickety seat, was the mass of honeysuckle.

If I had stood up and looked back, I would have seen the cottage; and if I had been on the bridge above the cottage and looked across the valley, I would have seen the top of the elder tree, bare branches in winter, green in spring and summer. In front of us on that September morning, across the bracken-covered moorland, we looked upon the standing stone and the rugged cliff rocks of Carn Barges; and the sea.

'This is where I want to be when I die,' said Jeannie, 'left wild as it is now, untamed.'

'Me too.'

It was an appropriate place. Carn Barges, where we had stood, seeing the cottage for the first time, standing there in excitement, visioning our future. Carn Barges would be there to watch us when the story was over.

Jeannie

The Carn has significance for Jeannie and me because when standing beside it after walking along the track from Lamorna Cove, we first saw the grey stone cottage of Minack; and had this powerful intuitive feeling that it held our future . . . When at last we had shaken off the shackles of our comfortable though exciting life in London, we experienced this exquisite feeling of relief. No waking up in the early

hours and being appalled at the prospect of the programme that filled the day ahead, no mental inquests, real or imaginary, of what went wrong the day before, no fears of plots among envious colleagues, no noise, no time-keeping, no stress artificially created by one's own imagination. The Carn, standing there, part of our landscape as we move around Minack, is the emblem of the freedom that we relish.

The Winding Lane

The cherry tree was now burgeoning into flower, a huge pink cushion; and when one early morning Jeannie and I took a walk to Carn Barges, we stood there looking back across the moorland to the cottage. The sun was rising behind us, and it was shining upon this huge pink cushion which was the cherry tree. Eleven months of waiting; and now for a month the cherry tree would have its time of glory.

The Cherry Tree

Blackthorn alley has the blackberry brambles on one side and the sloes on the other. It is a narrow path, and it has to be kept cut down to keep it open, and that is part of the charm of it. It is secret. Here foxes and badgers walk, and those who seek solitude; and there is no pounding of organised walkers aiming to go from one point to another on the map, pouting complaints if the walk involved does not represent a town pavement. Here in the blackthorn alley is mystery. I can be aware of life's subtlety. I can be aware of the opposites. I can look back on the scene of Minack, on the incidents which have woven themselves into the lives of Jeannie and myself, on the calmness its environment has given us in times of distress; and on the luck that led us to a way of life that we could share together.

The Evening Gull

The full moon was waiting to greet us at Minack, a soft breeze came from the sea and the Lizard light winked every few seconds across Mount's Bay. An owl hooted in the wood and afar off I heard the wheezing bark, like a hyena, of a vixen. A fishing boat chugged by, a mile off shore, its starboard light bright on the mast. It was very still. The boulders, so massive in the day, had become gossamer in the moonlight, and the cottage, so squat and solid, seemed to be floating in the centuries of its past.

I said to Jeannie: 'Let's see if Monty will come for a walk.'

He came very slowly down the lane, peering suddenly at dangers in the shadows, sitting down and watching us, then softly stepping forward. His white shirt-front gleamed like a lamp. He sniffed the air, his little nose puzzling the source of the scents of water weeds, bluebells and the sea. He found a log and clawed it, arching his back. He heard the rustle of a mouse and he became tense, alert to pounce. I felt as I watched him that he was an adventurer prying his private unknown, relishing the prospect of surprise and of the dangers which would be of his own making. We paused by the little stream, waiting for him to join us, and when he did, he rubbed his head affectionately against my leg, until suddenly he saw the pebbles of moonlight on the water. He put out a paw as if to touch them.

'I'll pick him up and carry him over.'

But when I bent down to do so he struggled free of my grasp—and with the spring of a panther he leapt across, and dashed into the shadows beyond.

'Well done!' we cried, 'well done!'

This little stream where it crosses the lane as if it were the moat of Minack, halting the arrival of strangers, greeting us on our returns, acting as the watch of our adventures, was given a name that night.

Monty's Leap.

We sat on the rock for a while, feet dangling, Ambrose between us, purring. A granite slab of rock, aeons old.

'An Everest moment,' said Jeannie.

Jeannie's definition of an Everest moment is when a long-awaited occasion totally measures up to expectation.

'Do you know what I'm going to call this rock?' went on Jeannie.

Another name for her to invent.

'What is it to be?' I asked.

'The Ambrose Rock.'

'An Everest moment . . . the Ambrose Rock. Yes, I see the connection.'

'I'll never for the rest of my life forget this moment,'Jeannie said, 'and I'll come and touch the Ambrose Rock and relive it.'

The Ambrose Rock has become a talisman for us. Indeed we sometimes treat it as if it was a wishing-well. We touch it and wish, as if we believe there is a link between ourselves and the timeless watchfulness of the rock which gives it a secret power.

Jeannie, however, has always been in the habit of making wishes. When there is a new moon, for instance, a sliver of light in the night sky, she will perform strange antics, bowing three times to the new moon, turning round three times, blowing a kiss three times, each time secretly making her wish.

I also play the wishing game but I do not always keep my wishes secret. On this occasion when we reached the rock I touched it and made a wish. Then Jeannie asked me what wish I had made.

'I wish for a quiet year,' I replied, rubbing the palm of my hand against the rough granite.

A Quiet Year

I did not go straight to the stable meadow. Instead I walked the few paces from the cottage door up the incline to the bridge, the patio which resembles the bridge of a ship as you stand there looking out upon the sea of Mount's Bay, the line of the Lizard stretching out like a pointing figure in the distance. I have spent much time there, still do, thinking over problems; or sometimes I stand there with my mind blank, wasting time a practical person might say, and yet wisdom may emerge from such silent moments. Thoughts come welling up from within you, spontaneously, often surprising you.

Jeannie

In tranquil moments, the bridge is a wonderful place to be. I have spent many hours there just staring, thinking of nothing except to observe the movement of a fox, or the lazy flight of a buzzard; or watching the purposeful voyaging of a trawler towards Newlyn, or looking above me at the long plume of an air liner on its way across the Atlantic; or listening to the hum of bees among the pink flowers of the escallonia which borders the bridge, or wondering why the gulls were crying; or experiencing the sudden delight of remembering a moment when Monty, Lama, or Oliver had suddenly decided to join me on the bridge, rubbing against a leg.

Standing quietly on the bridge places living in perspective. The riches lie within oneself, if one has the discipline to discover them . . . It will always be the individual who will be able to create his own happiness. Ideas from others may help him find it. But no one, no politician, no do-gooder, no priest, can solve the tortuous, conflicting thoughts of the individual, except himself.

The Ambrose Rock

The grey rocks and the old stones of the barn are ethereal in moonlight. It is a fairyland where pixies might suddenly appear; and the lane leading to Monty's Leap is touched with silver and, if you are in the mood to do so, you see the ghosts of past inhabitants of Minack, of old horses and cattle, of carts and haywains, and you regain in your imagination the leisurely pace of other ages.

Sun on the Lintel

There was one moonlight night shortly before Christmas when Lama wanted to go out, and I escorted her up to the Lama field. Across the bay were the sparkling lights of Porthleven, and the flooded lights of Culdrose, and those of the upturned mushroom dishes of Goonhilly pointing towards their Satellites. A glorious, keen night, salty sea air to breathe, a myriad stars winking above me, and silence. No passing boat to break the silence, no aircraft screaming, only the murmur of waves on rocks and the sudden coughing bark of a dog fox to remind me the natural world was continuing as it has done since the beginning.

A Cat Affair

We can go out of the cottage and shout to the heavens and no one will hear; or lie on the rocks with only cormorants, oyster catchers and gulls as companions; or stroll in the wood with Charlie hopping from branch to branch above our heads, or pause to talk to Tim, or say to each other; 'The gannets are passing along the coast early this year'...'I saw the first whitethroat this morning'... 'If you look to the left of those quickthorns you will see a fox sunning itself in the bracken'... 'The Seven Stones lightship was towed past this morning'... 'We'll have lunch on the rocks and watch the seal in the bay'...

A Gull on the Roof

The sun had now broken through the haze and it dazzled a path on the sea, silhouetting the rocks below me, hiding in darkness the gulls that were perched there, so that I heard them squawking without seeing them. Aeons of time and here was the same scene, the same etched lines of the rocks, the same language of the gulls, the same celandines, rose-pink campions, bluebells, wild violets around me, the same greening of the elder trees, the same white of the blackthorn, the same young ferns, the same bridal sprays of the sweet-scented sea-sandwort on grassy banks. A morning to be aware of one's luck. A morning to shout one's gratitude to the heavens. A morning to sympathise with those on trains and buses crowding into cities, or those passing through the factory gates to join the din of machinery. Here was peace. Here was the ultimate which man seeks. Nothing in a supermarket, nothing which could come from the success of a wage claim, nothing that a millionaire could buy, nothing that greed or envy could win, equals the reward of a spring morning on a lonely Cornish cliff; so quiet that you are truly at one with nature, listening to the sea touching the rocks, sinking one's mind into unplanned beauty.

Sun on the Lintel

I was up early in the morning, a glorious, hazy, warm May morning, and went down to the rocks for a bathe. Fishing boats, a half mile offshore, were hurrying to Newlyn market and gulls swirled in their wake. Two cormorants on the other side of the little bay, black sentinels in the sunlight, were standing on a rock regally surveying the scene; and on my left, up in the woods of the cliff, wood pigeons cooed. The scent of the sea filled the air, crystals sparkled the water, and the sound of the lazy, lapping waves was like a chorus of ghosts telling the world to hush. No angry engines in the sky disturbed the peace of it. No roar of traffic dulled the senses. Here was the original freedom. Here was poised a fragment of time when the world was young.

A Donkey in the Meadow

These belong to the pleasures which have pleased since the beginning of time. They await in remoteness, hiding their secret in solitude, unhurt by man-made glitter and away from his intrigue, seemingly insignificant moments which enrich the soul. They live with us at Minack so that whatever material disappointments we may have, however hard may be the consequences of a failed harvest, they take us forward again. It is a way of life which belongs to the ages instead of ourselves.

A Gull on the Roof

We are both romantics; and in the use of the word romantic I am embracing the pleasure gained by those slight, honest moments in life

31

that touch the heart, creating a sudden glow which surprises. Such moments may appear to be trivial in the view of the pundits, yet they have their value. They relax those who can enjoy them.

The Cherry Tree

Our pleasures were not designed for us at great expense by others. We had only to go and look out of the door, and whether the sun shimmered the Lizard in haze, or a raging storm thrust the foam and the waves into a darkening, winter sky, or the moon silvered the grey rocks that heaped around the cottage into the illusion of fairyland, we had only to see these things to shout to the heavens that we were alive. The sea breathed into our souls, the wind talked. We were part of the ageless striving of the human being. There around us, reflecting from the rough granite grey stones fingering up the walls of the cottage, were the calls of haymakers and the echo of carthorses, fishermen bringing their catch to the door, centuries of truthful endeavour, blazing summers, gales sweeping in from the south, justice in uncomplicated judgement, babies born and wagons carrying the old. All this we were aware of. All this elated every moment of our life at Minack.

All this was our stronghold.

A Donkey in the Meadow

A day lent . . . and Oliver and I took the track down the Merlin cliff; each meadow resembling a giant stepping-stone, each meadow showing the green spires of the daffodils that, within a month, should be in bloom, until I reached the blue elvan rock, partly covered by ivy, half-way down the track. There, because the day was warm and I felt idle, and there are times in life that you are able to smother inhibitions and enjoy pleasure without suffering a sense of guilt, I sat down. I sat down on the rock and, within a few seconds, Oliver had jumped on my lap; an uncomfortable lap because I was sitting at an angle. He gave a miniature yap, looked at me, then began to purr. I sat there, gulls gently gliding in the sky, the Bucks below us . . . I sat there on the blue elvan rock with Oliver purring on my lap, my mind far, far away from wrecks and stormy seas. There was no logical sequence in my thoughts. I was in one of those rare, hazy moods when the mind is unaffected by immediate problems and you find yourself roaming over a multitude of haphazard ideas which come welling up from the subconscious . . .

When the Winds Blow

Stay still, and I see the microscopic details of the kingdom. Stay still, and I am aware of the sounds that I haven't heard before, of the movement of insects that I haven't seen before, and of the wonder in the world that awaits our attention without relevance to the pay packet, or one-upmanship, or the greed for power. Stay still, and I can become aware of my secret self, difficult though it may be.

The Winding Lane

The grass path was barely a foot wide, bluebells crowding either side, and the tiny flowers of the stitchwort were scattered among them. Infant bracken was beginning to show, their fronds curled, resembling a baby's fist. Gorse, their cushions of golden petals hiding the spiky leaves, at intervals, wafted their scent. A lark was singing above the fields inland to my left and to my right among the scrubland a whitethroat burst into a frenzied chattering. I looked for it and saw it perched on a bramble; and I marvelled that this tiny bird, which a few weeks before was in North Africa, had now taken up its summer home on a Cornish cliff.

It is an incident like that which makes me want to worship not God but Creation.

A Quiet Year

The day was very still and the sounds we heard belonged to stillness: the mew of a buzzard high in the sky, a magpie chattering, a sudden brief song of a robin, the throb of a fishing boat on her way to Newlyn, the sound of our feet on the lane. There was the sweet knowledge of privacy as we walked, at that hour of the morning at that time of year no one was likely to suddenly appear. There are those who shun privacy, preferring the noise and activity of the herd. Others value privacy beyond price.

A Quiet Year

It was a crisp day, flaky clouds in the sky, and a breeze ruffling the sea. A few miles offshore, two massive deep-sea trawlers, curse of the local fishermen, patrolled slowly westwards, their fishing gear sucking up fish like a vacuum cleaner. In Mount's Bay, to the east, was anchored a Dutch tug, waiting for news of some vessel in distress to which it could rush, like a spider waiting for a fly to be caught in its web. Around us on the cliff was tranquillity. Yellow flecks of winter gorse, the pleasant scent of young nettles, dog violets showing between the rows of the daffodil beds, the occasional primrose in bloom before its time, waves below us swaying against the rocks, their foam like Cornish cream, and suddenly a flight of curlews veering momentarily out to sea when they saw us, then on eastwards towards Lamorna, calling their magical cries.

When the Winds Blow

Now here we were again years later, about to have a picnic breakfast close to where we dug the potatoes, and nothing had really changed. The rocks stared at the sea, the sea churned at the rocks. A cormorant was drying its wings on the other side of our teaspoon of a bay. Primroses were in clumps. Blackthorn was coming into white bridal flower in inaccessible places along the cliff. We were, as in the

36

beginning, blissfully happy, and Jeannie in her looks had been untouched by time. More than ever we were aware that if one is to have solid happiness, one has to have roots, then build on them. The roots will be there to comfort you in time of trouble.

We sat on a grass bank ... Jeannie spread butter on a slice of bread, covered it with tongue and handed it to me; and as she did so a scene in the previous night's television news passed through my mind: a scene showing rows of madmen screaming into telephones, each with a miniature television screen in front of them. Screaming madmen of London, New York and Tokyo manipulating the world's money markets.

But for Jeannie and me we were sharing a halcyon moment of idleness that reached into our souls.

Jeannie

Jeannie and I were on our own at Christmas; and when Geoffrey set off at lunchtime on Christmas Eve to have fun with his family, we opened a bottle of champagne and toasted the holiday to come. No decisions to make, an embargo on trying to solve problems, no cause to move away from the environment of Minack. This was a sweet moment. The world would peal its bells, the people worship in their churches, and boisterous bodies would dance and shout, wearing paper hats and throwing streamers, and television programmes would yell their jollity; but here it would be quiet. Clouds skimming over the Bay, a gull crying on the roof, a magpie chattering in the wood, a fan of wind breathing through the trees, a woodpecker laughing at dusk, and the sea murmuring, always the sea murmuring.

A Cat Affair

Here was the setting, the everlasting setting of Christmas; unabashed affection for each other, age no hindrance, the intellect momentarily defeated and emotion for the time being supreme, hard men kind, the mean pushed to display generosity, jealousy in abeyance, greed despicable, heightened awareness towards those you love, tenderness towards those taken for granted. This was the ancient shine which suffused the cottage as we laughed and rejoiced and shouted our way through Christmas dinner.

Lama

'I was thinking,' I said, after Merlin had given me another nudge in the back to tell me to walk faster, 'that most of the basics which make up happiness are corny.'

I had spoken, looking ahead, and Jeannie behind me, behind two donkeys as well, only heard a mumble.

'Speak up. I couldn't hear.'

'Most of the basics of happiness are corny.'

'And what does that mean?'

'Telling other people how to live their lives is an industry politicians, the media, academics, intellectuals, the churches, they are all part of the industry. And to keep the industry prosperous, they drench the public with their theories, confusing the public, leading them away from the obvious.'

The donkeys had stopped. A clump of out-of-season campion was being devoured.

'Go on.'

'The theories have to be complicated ones to keep the industry on the move; always promising results in the future, material or spiritual . . . and the obvious is ignored.'

'Which is?'

'The obvious revolves around the corny qualities of love and kindness.'

We were moving again and nearing Carn Barges, where we turn right and start on the final homeward stretch.

'You see, that's what I mean. Happiness is based on corny virtues. That is its weakness. It is too simple for this complicated world . . . and it provokes giggles. Some people are

39

always ready to giggle at simplicity.'

I heard the laugh of Jeannie behind me.

'As simple and corny,' she said, 'as taking two donkeys for a walk along a cliff!'

When the Winds Blow

'All life,' I said, 'except this instant is a dream.'

'Why do you suddenly say that?'

I was standing in a tiny meadow which borders an area of blackthorn within which are the homes of both a fox and a badger family. One of the most desirable sites in Cornwall, we say, because they are safe from the humans who would like to kill them. Jeannie was beside me; and Lama was squat at our feet, black tail round her paws, swaying her head, utterly at peace.

'Well,' I answered, 'what do you remember of this morning?'

'I got your breakfast, the post came, I wrote a letter to my sister, I wrote half a page of my book . . .'

'All hazy now in your mind.'

'I suppose so.'

'That's what I mean. Half one's life is dreaming of the future, the other half dreaming of the past.'

'I understand.'

'Our sophisticated years are now a dream, all the times at the Savoy, a bottle of champagne on ice in our room, a first night . . . Cholmondeley House, Thames Bank Cottage, glamorous parties in your office with Danny Kaye and all the others. Only the instant was permanent.'

'Like now.'

'Yes . . . you and I and Lama, and that robin, and the gull sailing down into the bay, and that wave moving in to smack the rocks . . . this is the instant which is real.'

Jeannie laughed.

'And now it's over!' she said.

I was being too serious, and she was bringing me back to my senses.

'All I was meaning,' I finished by saying, 'is that one mustn't take these instants for granted.'

A Cat Affair

'We're lucky,' I said. 'Lucky, lucky.'

We paused by the little cave where first Lama, then Oliver was born. It was not really a cave. It was a gap between two great rocks, and the narrow top was covered by a mass of ivy so that it was dark inside, and dry.

I laughed.

'I wonder how many times we have spoken that word,' I said.

'Thousands!'

In a world in which so many people are chained to routines they detest, or waste the hurrying days of their lives protesting against imaginary injustices, or conscientiously live their years but fail to fulfil their youthful dreams, it is sensible to appreciate one's luck.

A Cat Affair

ONE'S OWN HARD WORK

I was aware, on the other hand, that an idle time of staring and contemplation and living in the present, could only be justified if you had earned it. I knew, for instance, that our own pleasure this summer had been derived from experiences of things past, by efforts laboriously made, by all the failures, by successes which had suddenly pushed us forward without pushing us too far. Thus we had been able to pause, and live a dream without being so far from reality to deceive ourselves that it could last forever.

A Cornish Summer

I remember the first of those meadows. We still lived in London but Minack had become tentatively ours in the sense that our friend Harry Laity allowed us to be his tenants. We travelled down whenever we could for a few days; and on one of the earliest visits Jeannie and I became childishly excited because we found a pocket of ground which obviously, long ago, had been a cultivated meadow.

It was right at the bottom of the cliff, edging the last drop to the sea; so when we stood in the shadow of its once-cared-for cultivation, we could look down on the waves when the tide was high, or on rocks and shallow pools when it was low. One side there was an ancient stone wall, on another a high elderberry hedge; and in the centre was the meadow itself, chest high in undergrowth yet seemingly shouting at us to recognise it. Ghosts were there. Old men with sickles, blazing sunshine, parched soil, gulls' cries, tempests raging, forgotten harvests, a wren's song, badgers playing, the scent of primroses on soft spring mornings. We saw this hint of a meadow, and for a glorious two days Jeannie and I with the insane urge of enthusiasm ripped the undergrowth away, broke up the roots, and before we hurried back to civilisation, stared at the sweet earth, thankful for its reality.

A Drake at the Door

April passed, the potato season drew near and the inhabitants of the district, including ourselves, began to develop the mood of prospectors in a gold rush.

Three and four times a day Jeannie and I inspected the land which Tommy Williams had planted with one and a half tons of seed—the small meadows he had cut out of the top of the cliff; and the upper part of the cemetery field. The sight fascinated us. We stood and stared at the dark green leaves, hypnotised by their coarse texture, greedily calculating the amount of the harvest; then we would bend down and

46

tickle a plant, stirring the earth round it with our hands, and calling out when we found a tiny potato . . .

'Need a nice shower,' Tommy would say, 'and they'll treble in size within a week.' Or in the lane, I would meet John who, in answer to the inevitable question: 'How are the taties looking?' would say gloomily, 'Been known for a gale to come at this stage . . . blast them black and only the weight of seed been lifted.' It was not only the size of the harvest which was at stake, but also its timing. There was a rivalry among growers as to who would be the first to draw, like jockeys at the starting gate; and the information that was circulated was as inspired as that on a racecourse. I would go up to Jim Grenfell's pub at St Buryan in the evening and listen to the gossip.

'Bill Strick was cut by frost last night.'

'Over at Mousehole they look handsome.'

'Nothing will be going away until after Buryan Feast.'

'William Henry starts drawing Monday.'

These rumours and false alarms increased as the pace of excitement grew faster every day, and by the end of the month the inevitable question had become: 'Started drawing yet?'

A Gull on the Roof

It was very hot those first two months at Minack, and it was like a furnace down the cliff as we dug our early potatoes. We often worked together on our own and, because the ambiance of the beautiful scenery and its loneliness made us feel we were on a South Sea island, Jeannie would be naked as she picked up the potatoes while I, wearing boots, dug them up with my long-handled Cornish shovel.

Then after a while, Jeannie would suddenly say she had had enough and was going to have a bathe; and she would run away from me, down the foot-wide track to the rocks and the sea. I would watch her, this gazelle-like creature, and ponder how such a short while ago she was daily playing the role of a sophisticated hostess at the Savoy or the Berkeley or Claridge's.

She would pause at the point where the track fell steeply and took her out of sight. She would pause, and wave at me, her long dark hair falling over her bare shoulders. A few seconds later, gulls disturbed from their somnolent ruminating, rose from the rocks calling their weird cries; and telling me that Jeannie had arrived at the rock pool where she bathed.

Jeannie

The bright light of day had gone from the cliff when we reached it and the sun was dipping to the sea on the other side of the Penwith peninsula. The shadows of the rocks were enjoying their brief passage of life before dark, and the sea was dotted with the waking lights of the pilchard fleet. I poised the long-handled shovel and cumbersomely jabbed it under a plant, lifting the bundle of earth and tossing it to where Jeannie was standing. She stooped, shook the sturdy leaves, and ran her hand through the soil. And there, gleaming bright in the dusk were six potatoes, each the comfortable size of a baby's fist.

Jeannie and I were up at dawn the following morning and I drove the Land Rover over the shoulder of the cemetery field and down to the top of the cliff. It was a heavenly morning with a haze hiding the horizon, the first swallows skimming the landscape, the white parasols of the may trees pluming from the green bracken, and the scent of the bluebells mingling with the salt air of the sea. In the back of the car we had a spring balance weighing machine and a tripod on which to hang it, a bundle of chips and a ball of binder twine with which to tie the cardboard tops when the chips were full, a pair of scissors, the shovel, a box full of salesman's labels with printed addresses of different markets. It was a lush moment of hope blissfully blinded from the realities the years would see.

A Gull on the Roof

It is a sweet moment when a long-awaited harvest awakes. It shares the common denominator of pleasure which embraces all endeavours that have taken a long time to plan, to nurture, and then suddenly bursts before your eyes in achievement. You are no longer an onlooker waiting impatiently. The harvest is there to give you your reward; the fact of it destroys your worries and galvanises you into action. I know of few things so evergreen sweet as the first picking of a new crop.

A Drake at the Door

We awoke as tired as when we went to bed, limbs aching, our minds fogged by our dreams and the prospect of another day of chain gang labour. I would get up and put the kettle on the paraffin stove and when it had boiled replace it with a saucepan for the eggs. Then, breakfast over, we would walk along the path to the top of the cliffs where the chips in neat rows awaited their weighing, and suddenly, as if an icepack had melted miraculously before our eyes, we became aware of the glory of the early morning. We looked down on to the sea, glittering from the sun which rose above the Lizard, spattered with fishing boats hurrying to the Newlyn fish market like office workers scurrying to town. A cuckoo flew past, topping the undergrowth, calling as she went. A cormorant perched on the rock that is called Gazell, its black wings extended, drying them against the softness of the breeze. High in the sky a wood pigeon courted another, clapping its wings, then swooping silently and up again, and another clap as sharp as a pistol shot. Around us bluebells brimmed the green grass and foxgloves pointed to the sky like sentinels. Meadow sweet and may blossom clung on the air with their scent. A woodpecker laughed. And the sea, sweeping its cool tranquillity to the horizon, lapped its murmur against the rocks below us. Here was the heightened moment when the early morning, unspoilt like a child, is secure from passing time; and when a human being, sour with man-made pleasures, awakes to the sweet grace of freedom.

A Gull on the Roof

There was such joy in those moments: here was the moment of personal achievement, the realisation of a reward that millionaires cannot buy. We had turned the ground in the autumn, we had bought the seeds, 'shot' them in a hut till their sprouts appeared, then planted them, watched them peep through the soil, then hoed them, been anxious about them, worrying whether storm or frost might destroy them . . . and now it was all over. They were on their way to market.

Jeannie and I were besotted by potatoes at this period. Our livelihood, and our future, depended upon them. I kept a log book, and its contents reflect our tunnel-vision attitude towards potatoes. There is no mention of other events in our lives. No descriptions of sights around us. No record of those who visited us. Just an endless record of our infatuation with potatoes.

Jeannie

The first winter I cared not a rap for such economic factors because my imagination did not wish to grasp the prospect that they would ever beset me. I was doped by the sheer pleasure of being a peasant; by the plodding work that did not require mental activity; by day-end exhaustion that did not repay with worried, sleepless nights; by the pleasure of achievement after I had defeated the wind and the rain, and the baskets were filled with violets.

Physical effort is so much more gentle than that of the mind and, being new to it, I found it more rewarding. Mine was the pleasure of the mountaineer, the Channel swimmer or the marathon runner—enthusiasm allied with determination that brought victory which is sweet to the senses and provided tangible conquest in a personal battle. I was blessed at the time by the simple belief that flower growing was determined by obeying certain well defined rules, and success was automatic for him who did so; manure the ground, for instance, see there is enough lime, stick the plants in at the right time, and so on. I had, of course, to work hard and be ready to accept advice from experienced growers whenever I was in doubt, and pick their brains whenever I had the chance. I had, in fact, to behave like any intelligent man with initiative, and my reward would be flowers in abundance. I had not the slightest conception of the savage surprises ahead of me, nor of the bewildering contradictions that growing provides.

A Gull on the Roof

We needed, however, that good harvest the first year; and our optimism excited us to expect it. It was indeed vital that it should be a good one. The hazy honeymoon with escapism was being replaced by the conventional necessities of day to day existence, our commitments were increasing, our reserves dwindling. We took on Pentewan knowing it would vastly increase our expenses, but saying to ourselves that if we planned with vision, courage and care, all we would then require would be to have luck on our side; for endeavour, however painstakingly pursued, can rarely receive its accolade unless a magic bestows it.

Yet we were aware that there was something else at stake besides material victory; there was the continuing challenge to prove that we were not flirting with the tedium of manual labour, that our enthusiasm had not been checked by reverses or by the roughness of the life, that we possessed staying power which could earn respect. It was a simple ambition and some would call it a valueless one, but within it there was the prospect of peace of mind born of permanence. There is no permanence in the conventional ambitions that hasten you up the pyramid of power, each step killing one ambition and creating another, leading you by a noose to a pinnacle where, too late, you look back on the trampled path and find the yearning within you is the same as when you were young.

We knew, therefore, that we could not

impose ourselves on the countryside but had to be absorbed by it, creating by our efforts an intangible strength that became an element of the beauty, of the wildness, and of the peace around us; and we would then begin to feel and to see the gossamer secrets that are for ever hidden from the casual passer-by.

A Gull on the Roof

There was the beauty of the work as well. Tiredness, as known in other spheres, had no chance to conquer when the senses were being constantly refreshed by the tangible evidence of spring. Each morning we would enter the wood; then stop and marvel before we began to pick. Overnight buds had dropped, opened and were peering their golden yellow over the green foliage, each with a destiny to provide delight. It was like a ballroom of child dancers, innocent and exquisite, brimmed with an ethereal happiness, laughing, loving, blind to passing time; and yet, almost unnoticed, day by day the flowers were leaving, then gathering speed, until suddenly there was only a floor of green, flecked here and there by a bloom that had stayed behind. The dance was over.

A Gull on the Roof

It was a sweet spring. No gales seemed to threaten us, and following the bitter winter the various varieties leapt forward together as soon as the earth was warmed. It was a bumper crop, every bulb burst into bloom instead of the customary misses, and Minack meadows were covered with potential income. And when these meadows are yellow against the backdrop of a deep blue sea even the cynic will marvel, even the man whose salary is derived from destroying by words or by vision, even the devil would not deny it is one of the most beautiful sights in the world.

A Donkey in the Meadow

The shadows fall early on our cliff. The setting sun is still comparatively high behind the hill when the rocks begin to point their fingers towards the sea. It becomes cool when on the top of the hill it is still warm. You soon have a sense of impending sleep, a settling for the night as the confetti of gulls drift against the dying sky, floating to smooth rocks, calling from time to time. I would then carry the baskets we had filled up the steep path to the field, load them into the Land Rover, and the two of us would drive up the field and along the track to Minack. The same track, the same view awaiting us, as when years before, at a moment of despair, we looked ahead of us, and Jeannie called out as if our problems had been solved: 'Look! There's a gull on the roof!'

A Donkey in the Meadow

All day we would bunch. It is one of the most soothing tasks you could wish for, and as each bunch is completed and you hold it up and look at it to make quite sure that each bloom is perfect, you experience the naïve pleasure that within forty-eight hours it will be lighting up a room; and you feel you are lucky indeed to be performing a task which earns such a reward.

A Donkey in the Meadow

There is an aspect of the daffodil season which never fails to give pleasure. Jeannie and I could wake up in the morning and know that we would not be embarking upon a task during the coming day which was destructive, morally or physically. Every bunch of daffodils would soon be decorating a corner of some far-away room, soothing a sensitive person, lighting up their minds, calming them, exciting them into being reminded that the basic values of happiness always remain the same.

Jeannie

They could not imagine they had come from meadows overlooking the sea of Mount's Bay; meadows bounded by blue elvan rocks and thick hedges of blackthorn; meadows with trowel-shaped holes where a badger had been digging for a bluebell bulb; meadows where if you are picking in the early morning you catch the scent of a fox as you bend; meadows poised over a turbulent sea where a gannet might be diving unafraid; meadows so sheltered by ancient stone hedges and rock formations that you can stand there untouched by the wind or by a gale which roars at you when you leave the peace of the cliff. In such meadows we picked the *obvallaris* for Harrods ... natural daffodils of the cliffs which had been growing there for decade upon decade.

A Quiet Year

When we finished the bunching we gathered the discarded blooms, the crooked ones and the short ones, those with damaged petals and warped petals, and brought them into the cottage for our own pleasure; and the others stood in their jars waiting for the morrow when Jeannie would pack them in their long cardboard boxes, and no doubt would call me because she could never take the beauty for granted: 'Come and see this box. It's special!'

The Way to Minack

This was the first vision . . . the idyllic present, freedom from employer responsibility, being absorbed by one's own hard work, undeterred by long hours because one was being exhilarated by one's own achievement. Bunches of daffodils which would give pleasure to homes in city streets. Pride in the contents of every daffodil box we despatched. Satisfaction at the day's end. Crossing our fingers that our luck would hold. The luck of being able to live the kind of life we loved.

The Winding Lane

'You give something to the flower trade, you two.'

I believe when he said this that both of us felt so emotional that we wanted forcibly to restrain him from leaving us. He had given us the key. He had made no deliberate effort to do so but his antennae, without which a talented person will be ordinary, had sensed we needed a lift. And we were able excitedly and so happily to respond. Here was an instant of good luck without which no endeavour can succeed; and the only issue at stake was taking advantage of it . . .

We knew also that we must not betray all the struggle, sacrifice, and enthusiasm which led the way to us receiving such a compliment. We must attack. This collision between despondency and the praise we had received was a reflection of all the years we had been at Minack. The earth and the rain and the wind may have hurt us but they had never, I felt, dimmed the truth of our optimism. We struggled where we loved. Failure was in the hands of the gods, not in the hands of human beings. When we fought for our survival, we did not have to weary ourselves waiting upon the whims of other people. We were alone. We were together.

'Jeannie,' I said, such relief in my mind and the enthusiasm simmering again which had been curbed in the tight circle of wavering defeatism, 'let's give ourselves one more chance!'

A Donkey in the Meadow

The glut caught us by surprise. Gluts always do. It is a penalty of not having a telephone. We refuse to have a telephone because we find that an ingredient for enjoying a country life is to try to live it as it was lived in time past; and in time past there was no ringing bell to interrupt the day, no threat of a ringing bell. When we lived in London it was very different. I was a telephone king, and Jeannie was a telephone queen. Hours were spent gossiping, which often meant saying things one should not have said, and regretting them later; or accepting invitations which, if they had come by letter, one would have had time to reflect upon and refuse; or, more dangerously, seizing the telephone because some event had made one indignant. We were now spared such hazards. We were spared those anxiety questions: 'Will you answer it?' or 'Has anyone rung?' And the penalty we had to pay for such

61

tranquillity was, momentarily, to be unaware of the glut.

When the Winds Blow

It took a fortnight to erect the greenhouse; and when it was completed Jeannie and I used to stand inside for an hour on end, gazing in wonderment. It was our personal Crystal Palace. The expanse of it, the heat of the sunshine despite the cold winds outside, the prospect of now being able to grow crops without the endless threat of the elements, produced such excitement that we bought a bottle of champagne and christened it.

A Drake at the Door

We were absorbed in the work. We had paid help, in those days: someone to keep the routine moving when we might be otherwise engaged, but we were never just observers. We would spend hours at a time on our knees, picking the weeds from the whalehide pots which contained the freesias, and I would water them and water the chrysanths and the bulbs; dreamily dangling the hose along the rows of pots. I had no thought of writing in

62

those days; nor did Jeannie. Our minds were in suspension. We were discovering the delights of being free from mental responsibilities, the delights of being manual workers, the extraordinary pleasures that can be obtained by those who do not have to make big decisions. Pick, pick, pick out the weeds. Hose this whalehide pot sufficiently, hose that one, hose this one. The relaxation of working without using our brains was ours.

Yet such an attitude on our part was a delusion. We were indulging ourselves as we picked out the weeds and watered the pots. We were only enjoying a respite from management. We still had to earn the money to pay the wages. We still had to pay for the pleasure of being our own masters, by taking risks, by finding the capital to pay for those risks.

When the Winds Blow

Weeds seem to me to provoke a form of horticultural class warfare. Weeds are belowstairs, flowers are abovestairs. I have often wondered how it was decided what should be flowers, and what should be weeds; and why it should be that, unlike the man-made social scene, weeds have never been able to edge their way upwards in the garden social scene. Why should the yellow of a dandelion be considered belowstairs? Or what is wrong with the purple flower of a knapweed unless one has long been brainwashed into believing that one has committed a social error by not pulling it up?

A Quiet Year

Placid-looking market gardeners are inveterate gamblers and their life is not, as it appears, a plodding one. It dwells in high excitement, and the charm of it is that the grey doubts of the future are invariably quelled by titillating prospects of a new season.

A Gull on the Roof

When I set off with the brush cutter to the cliff meadows, I always suffered from being controlled by Pisces, my birth sign. I always argue with myself as to which of the meadows I should begin cutting. I will wake up in the morning and say to Jeannie that I am going to cut the far meadows, then change my mind after breakfast, saying I am going down Minack cliff which meant I was going to cut the meadows which, with Tommy Williams, our eccentric, devoted, first helper, we first carved out of the untamed land that was to give us a livelihood. Once when he was pausing from digging up the potatoes, I saw him leaning on his long-handled Cornish shovel and heard him saying as if to himself as he stared out to sea: 'What more can a man want than a morning like this and a view like that?'

I move into a small meadow on a steep slope, the brush cutter slung across my shoulder, and begin weaving it to and fro like a scythe, the circular blade spinning at speed, the two-stroke engine roaring with a noise like that of a motorbike. I know every meadow so intimately that I will be aware that under one layer of bracken lies a clump of pink campion that flowers all through the winter, and so I will attack the bracken very delicately and save the pink campion. Violets also abound in these cliff meadows and I am always on the watch for them; and if by mistake I lop one off, I curse myself for doing it. I have to keep a look out, also, for an early primrose, and if I find a clump, I will switch off the brush cutter, lay it on the ground, then bend down to the clump and bury my face in the petals. When one is unobserved, one can behave at such moments in a very basic fashion.

A Quiet Year

These meadows to which we were going ... were our personal meadows. Every corner of them we knew. Every badger path which ran through them. Every half submerged rock. We had created them. We had slashed the undergrowth, turned the ground, and over the years we had worked them, digging potatoes on hot summer days, picking daffodils when elsewhere the country was covered with snow. They had also been part of our weakness, our refusal to move with the times.

A Quiet Year

I ... went up the cliff, pausing again just before I reached the little gate which led to Fred's field. I was staring downwards now, down at the turbulence of the sea, down at the fishing boats and the french crabber, down at the coaster and another one which had just come into view. And down, I realised, at my past.

For this cliff was the lure which led us away from our London lives; and on that day, sickle and scythe in our hands, when we began to slash order into the cliff, opening up again long-forgotten meadows and creating new ones, we truly believed that the world stood still. Machines? Horticultural industrialisation? We were so naïve that we never considered such things would interfere with our future, never considered the possibility of man-made over-production. Only the elements, we thought, would be our enemy; and when in due course we endured gales which pulverised our crops, or a sudden frost which destroyed six months' income in a night, we were comforted by the knowledge that nature had been the architect of our defeat, not man. Nature represented freedom, and could be forgiven; man, in contrast, offered chains, and more chains. Man's mistake is to believe that freedom is orderly.

Cottage on a Cliff

Below were the rocks, granite and blue elvan pitted with fissures, huge ungainly shapes each part of the whole which sloped without plan inevitably to the sea. Here the seaweed, draped like an apron, thickened the water at low tide; and gulls, oyster-catchers, and turnstones poked among it, uttering wild cries. There was the sense of loneliness, and yet of greatness. This was unmanageable nature, the freedom man chases.

And to us the cliff reflected our endeavour since we came to Minack. It was a part of ourselves. We had seen it those years ago when it was untamed, and visioned the meadows we would carve from the undergrowth, the rich crops we would grow, the sure future we would build. Here we had been a part of some victories and many defeats. We had seen harvests of early potatoes lashed by a gale and destroyed in a night. We had laboured on hot summer days on this cliff shovelling with the long-handled Cornish spade beneath the potato plants, Jeannie on hands and knees picking up the potatoes and filling the sacks, then the long steep climb to the top, a sack at a time, journey after journey.

We had rejoiced in the flower season at the sight of the daffodils, dazzling yellow against the blue sea, gulls high above, gannets plummeting offshore; then gladly endured the steady task of picking, gathering an armful and slowly filling a basket; and the climb again, heavy basket in either hand. Such as this was our victory. Here in remoteness, a sense of communion with the base of beauty. Not victory in a worldly sense. We produced. We were two of the losing originals. When our efforts left our environment, so did our control. Far away people, cool in their calculations, undisturbed by our hopes, beset with their own problems, decreed our reward.

We had our shield. Moments like the quiet of a Christmas morning when Jeannie and I were together, with a cat called Lama who was born within sound of the sea.

Lama

Meanwhile I was experiencing the glory of daffodil time, a time which used to be the most hectic period of the year, as we picked, bunched and despatched the boxes to market. In those days many of the meadows would have been bare of yellow by early March, and only the green foliage would be left; and the first daffodils we had picked and sent away would have been in dustbins. Not any more. The daffodils, as they swayed in the breeze, looked as if they were laughing, laughing that they were free, not to be sent away to be shown off in early morning markets, shown off in shops, pushed into vases, ending in dustbins. They were rejoicing because they were staying at home.

Monty's Leap

THE WORLD OF CREATION

A crisp, January morning; frost up country, but none at Minack since winter began. The wind is our enemy, our perpetual enemy. Frost makes darting attacks, ice on the water butt that has melted by noon. Frost is not a perpetual enemy like the wind; nor is snow. Frost and snow flirt with us; but when, year after year, we are lulled into thinking that the flirtation is harmless, they will suddenly cause us dismay. The pipe from the well is frozen, no bath water, no drinking water, and I have to take a pail to Monty's Leap and scoop from the stream . . .

No prospect of snow on this crisp, January morning; no prospect of frost. It is one of those clean Cornish winter days, when the horizon is clear and the sea sparkles in the sun and the gulls float above the cliffs, and early wallflowers scent their yellow petals.

When the Winds Blow

When Christmas is over and the New Year, a restful time begins at Minack. We are waiting for the daffodils, we have time on our own, and in January Cornwall belongs to its residents. and for them it becomes like a huge garden.

Roads are free of drivers who think they are

still on motorways, car parks are free of attendants, beaches are empty for gulls and other seabirds, one can walk for miles on the coastal path without seeing anyone coming towards one, and while one reads accounts of a harsh winter elsewhere, one rejoices in the dawning of spring. Courting ravens grunt at each other, coltsfoot perfumes the bank of a stream, a sudden primrose shines in a meadow and spikes of early daffodils show above ground. One is aware that the world is beginning again, not the man-made world but the world of Creation. It is a slow world which one watches. One has to have patience to see it, and feel it. It is the feeling of it which enriches the soul. Anyone can *see* the countryside. The lucky ones are those who have the time to be absorbed by it.

A Quiet Year

There are sounds at winter's end that a year's interval has made you forget; sights too, and scents. I forget that gulls' cries become urgent, more demanding. I forget the burble of a robin, silent for the previous months. I forget the sudden eruption of the blue tits, and the coal tits, flighting in branches around the cottage, expecting that I have nothing better to do than to throw sunflower seeds to them all day long. I forget the sweet scent of the heliotrope. I forget that nettles like tiny fists are growing again, that gorse is speckled with yellow petals that smell as if summer has come. I forget that the bracken in the croft land is so flat and dead that you cannot imagine it will ever be green again. I forget that there always comes a morning when the air is soft and the sun is shining, that the senses are suddenly deliciously aware of the coming of spring.

Jeannie

The spring came early the following year. In February there were gentle west winds, balmy days which sent the larks into the sky to sing a month before their time. The green woodpecker in the elms below the cottage clung to the bark tapping his note of joy, unperturbed that the splendour of his crimson crown among the bare branches was there for all to see. The sunshine was his safety.

There was a rush of wings in Minack woods. Exultant songs from the willows, blackbirds courting, and thrushes rivalling them with glorious notes. Harsh warbles from the chaffinches, and the trills of the wrens, fluffing their tiny bodies, then bellowing their happiness. Magpies coarsely cried. The two ravens from the cliff flew overhead coughing their comments on what they could see below.

Robins were careless in hiding their nests, no time for danger for spring was here. Owls hooted in the daylight. The wintering flocks of starlings gathered in the sky like black confetti wondering whether to leave. Too soon for the chiff-chaffs or the warblers or the whitethroats. They did not know we had an early spring. Minack woods still belonged to those who lived there.

The sea rippled in innocence, and when the *Scillonian* sailed by to and from the Islands we could hear in the cottage the pounding of her engines; for the wind and the surf were silent. Fishermen were tempted to drop their lobster pots, and one of them every day had a string across our tiny bay. There were others feathering for mackerel. Cockleshell white boats with men in yellow oilskins, engines chattering until the moment came to switch off and to drift with the tide. Gulls aimlessly dotted the water, like lazy holidaymakers. Cormorants on the edge of rocks held out their wings to dry like huge, motionless bats. The first primroses clustered on the cliff's edge and the white blooms of the blackthorn spattered the waste land above. A beautiful spring, only the task was to be part of it; but to us it held a threat.

A Drake at the Door

When disgruntled people in cities march to

meetings on May Day holding high their banners of protest, the white flowers of the blackthorn lie in drifts in Minack woods and along the shallow valley which slopes towards the sea.

Chunky patches of golden gorse line the lane to the farm at the top of the hill, blue periwinkle spatter the banks; late primroses, wild violets, and early pink campion shelter amidst the growing grass. Fields of our neighbours where they have sown spring corn are covered by a film of green; white blossom clusters on the pear tree which we planted two years ago; and by the wooden plank which crosses Monty's Leap, the sticky leaves of the trichocarpa exude their exotic scent.

Persian Carpet wallflowers colour the beds around the cottage. Aubretia, white and mauve, fall over moss-covered stones. Dandelions are beginning to prove their invincibility again, piercing the joints of the stones in the path outside the cottage door. Foolish bumble bees buzz against the glass of the porch. A cuckoo, dipping its tail, calls on the rock at Carn Barges. A vixen in the lane in the afternoon warns us that cubs have made her fearless. A wren sings among the willows beside the stream. The first bluebells are in flower down the cliff. A blackbird in the elderberry close to the barn proclaims that she has a nest nearby. Rabbits chase each other in the field opposite. Last year's tadpoles crawl as frogs from hibernating hideouts. The sunset is noticeably further to the west. Woodpigeons hurry to and from the wood, larks sing above the field behind the bridge, small birds perform aerobatics in their excitement, gulls' cries have an enlarged vocabulary. This is May Day.

A Cornish Summer

The sun was on the lintel, the massive rough granite lintel above the fireplace. It was no splash of sun. It was a shaft, the size of a fist.

'Summer has begun,' I said to Jeannie, who was in the kitchen preparing dinner.

The sun had moved far enough west for it to be setting below the hill of the donkey field; and as it dipped there came a moment when it filtered through the glass of the porch, through the open doorway, and touched the old stone. Each evening, each week, it moved across the lintel until high summer was over; and then back it would come, imperceptibly moving to the point where we had first seen it, and then it would vanish. Autumn, winter, spring would pass before we saw it again.

Sun on the Lintel

The lush period of summer had now begun.

Young green bracken was thrusting through the thickening grass, through the mass of leaves of the fading bluebells, draping the sides of lanes and blanketing the moorland, hiding paths which were once easy to find. Coarse docks and thistles sprouted in the daffodil meadows among the dying foliage of the daffodils. Ought we not to be efficient daffodil growers and keep the meadows sprayed with herbicides instead of relying on the motor mower in due course to cut them down? But we prefer to let the wild flowers be free, the good ones and the bad ones, and in June this summer the insects were humming in the meadows, butterflies stretched out their wings on useless weeds, chattering whitethroats clung to the thistles pecking at the first seeds. Up the lane from the cottage the stream had already become a trickle across Monty's Leap, the may tree beyond the gate on the right was a dome of white scented petals; nettles and foxgloves, Queen Anne's lace, clouds of pink campion and inevitable cow parsley filled the verges and the ditches. And the leaves were now thick on the branches of the elm where the nest of the mistlethrushes used to be, and on the branches around the woodpeckers' hole out of which the eldest one, at any moment, would be ready to fly.

Cornish Summer

The drought, the long hot summer, had made me languid. I would spend hours transfixed by tranquillity, a mood which stopped me from performing anything of importance. I became immersed in idleness. I would stare and listen, and be absorbed in that other dimension of life which hurrying man seldom has the time to enjoy.

The chuckle of a green woodpecker, for instance, coming from the wood, a bee settling on a blackberry flower, a lizard sneaking out of a crevice in the wall beside the verbena bush, pedestals of pennywort miraculously growing in finger nail shallow earth, ants from summer's beginning to summer's end marching in single line round the cottage past the blue water butt and around towards the porch neatly taking a route that skirted the bottom of the front door, a persistent churring of a whitethroat among the brambles and bracken surrounding the well, the aroma of a distant moorland fire, a flycatcher with dumpy chest pausing on an ash branch then darting at a cabbage white, the ground hard and slippery as ice so that I kept Fred on a halter as I walked him along the cliff path, Monty's Leap dried up, the small reservoir empty, the well water only pumping twenty gallons a day, curlews flighting across the valley, settling on the dried grass field opposite, calling all the while their sad cries, Red Admirals on ivy leaves, white moths in the evening fluttering around the night scented stock and the mauve and white tobacco plants, Ronald the rook chortling on the roof, Philip the old gull astride the glass roof of the porch stamping at it with his beak, vexed that I had painted it with white shading, stopping him from looking down at us as we sat inside, far travelling bees humming among the escallonia, yachts in Mount's Bay resembling toy boats on a pond, Charlie the chaffinch gobbling Jeannie's coconut cake, Charlie busy with his own family but also, this being so strange, feeding a young robin.

Such peaceful idleness, however, did not mean that we were living in a lotus land all day. We had the alarm clock ringing in our ears at five in the morning; and while it was still cool we did our work.

The Winding Lane

High summer, and the end is beginning. The elder flowers have turned into berries, the apples are fattening, the tomato plants have only the top trusses to ripen, the air sings with insect sounds, flies bother the donkeys, convolvulus is winding up the camellia bush beside the rose garden, up the fuchsia and the honeysuckle in front of the cottage, up any plant or bush it can find; bees fill themselves with honey from the mignonette on the bridge, multi-coloured nasturtiums tumble over rocks, night-scented stock and tobacco plants romanticise the evenings. There still seems much of summer ahead ... but the swifts are gathering, briefest of our bird visitors, and any evening they will be spiralling into the sky above Minack, calling their shrill cry of farewell, higher and higher, until they disappear in the fading light.

A Cornish Summer

It was a lovely morning. A morning that belonged to summer. A still sea, soft salty scents, a quiet sky. I could have believed it was a June morning except there were no swallows dancing in the sky or darting in and out of the barn door; and the bracken swathing the moorland was a red-brown instead of a rich green, and spider webs shimmered on the hedges, and the leaves of the elms had begun to fall in the wood, and buds were plumply showing on the December-flowering camellia bush. The year was lying about its age. It had produced this Indian summer to fool the Red Admiral butterfly that fluttered from leaf to leaf on the escallonia opposite the entrance to the cottage, and the blackbird which sang a spring song in the blackthorn near the well, and the fox I saw basking in a corner of the field on the other side of the shallow valley.

Cottage on a Cliff

The rains came in November. They came roaring in from the south, grey skies, grey seas, waterbutt overflowing flushing a channel in the grey chippings, pools on the stone path outside the door, donkeys with heads down and backs to the weather when they could be dry in the stable, land soggy, noisy restless trees, birds sheltering in the escallonia by the terrace we call the bridge, a gull clinging in the wind to the roof, all nature accepting the first punishment of winter.

Then suddenly a day, and the sky is blue brushed by fluffy white clouds, and it is unexpectedly warm, and I forget. Momentarily yesterday's storm is only in the imagination.

We have a day lent. The Indian summer continues.

Cottage on a Cliff

Michaelmas Day is the beginning of winter. The day when retiring farmers hand over to their successors, when beefy lifeguards have departed from now deserted beaches and holiday hotels have closed till another summer, when seashore car parks are empty and pampered gulls wonder what has happened, when ice cream kiosks are shuttered and the winds begin to blow, when some will grumble that life has become too quiet and others will be glad the holiday season is over: 'Cornwall belongs to Cornwall again.' The visitors have gone.

There are sleepy flies on the last blackberries, spider webs stretch across narrow paths, I flush the first woodcock from a patch of battered bracken as I walk towards Carn Barges, a fieldfare in the stable meadow below the cottage looks surprised to be in a strange country, a late wasp buzzes dozily against a window of the porch, blue-tits have returned to the bird-table after being self-sufficient during the summer, faded honeysuckle still blooms in odd places down the cliff a hundred yards the cliff a hundred yards away, ivy leaves are yellow-green and leaves of the brambles haveturned a robin-red. Wild violets are in clusters. Winter gorse is in flower.

I pull up an imaginary drawbridge at Monty's Leap when winter comes. I play a game that Jeannie and I live in a fortress with a deep moat surrounding us. We have no part in the busy, fractious, unsatisfied outside world, and nothing can disturb the easy motion of the day. Strikes, inflation, unemployment, violence, greed, envy, all these I pretend play no part in our lives. I have passing fantasies that peace of mind has been permanently obtained by looking after our own lives instead of interfering in the lives of others. I am therefore immune, I pretend, from the tedious troubles of the herd. I live in a world where time is mine. I am a countryman living in a remote place with the chance to keep my own identity. I am as simply happy as the uncomplicated peasant of a hundred years ago who never left his parish. Such a game I may play for a day, for two, for three: and then some incident will occur which wakes me up to reality.

Cottage on a Cliff

Winter had now become a companion. In the wood I found nests which I had not seen in summer. The bushes and trees were bare, and I suddenly discovered the tiny nest of the goldfinches who had haunted me in June and July with their bell-like chirruping, and darting red and gold. There it was in the hawthorn, just above me as I passed by Boris the drake's old hut, clusters of red berries now around it. A few yards away, within touching distance of the path, was a thrush's nest hidden in summer by the green leaves of the blackthorn; and cupped in the fork of another hawthorn was the nest of a chaffinch, and in the bank close to a magnolia was that of a robin and in the ivy that greedily climbed an ash-tree was a bundle of moss belonging to a wren, and in the willow were the dried sticks of a wood-pigeon's nest, and in one of the elms was the perfectly rounded hole of a green woodpecker who never stayed to use it. Winter unmasked summer.

Cottage on a Cliff

The winds curl Minack in winter. In the beginning while we sat snug in the cottage a sense of security acted as a narcotic against the roar outside. A book, a pipe, the scent of a wood fire, Monty on my lap, there was comfort in joining the ghosts who had listened to the same rage, in sheltering within the walls that withstood centuries of siege. Then as we passed through the shoals of first enthusiasm, facing the reality of the task we had undertaken, tension replaced comfort as the winds blew.

I am afraid now when the westerly comes galloping over the hill behind the cottage and charges with thundering hoofs into the elms that edge the wood; when the northerly steps aloofly along the valley, chilling its visit with frost; when the easterly bites from the Lizard, mouthing the sea and ripping our cliff which puts up a hand to stop it; when the southerly brings the rain and the storm which binds the sea and the land in gloom. For all are our enemies. Those from the east and the south carry salt as they blow, salt which films over flower petals and leaves and burns them papery white. That from the west savages the crops like a madman, that from the north shivers black the plants in its way.

A Gull on the Roof

Fishermen call the Lizard wind the starving wind, for the fish hide from it on the bed of the sea and the boats return empty to port. Landsmen solemnly call it the gizzard wind as it bites into the body and leaves you tired when the day is still young. It is a hateful wind, no good to anybody, drying the soil into powdery dust, blackening the grass like a film of oil, punching the daffodils with the blows of a bully. It is seldom a savage wind as it was on the night it destroyed the Hospodar and Coverack Glory; if it were, if it spat its venom then recoiled into quiet, you could cry over the damage and forget. Instead it simmers its fury like a man with a grudge, moaning its grievance on and on, day after day, remorselessly wearying its victims into defeat.

A Gull on the Roof

There was a sound outside as if a car was driving up to the cottage. 'Listen,' I said, and we paused, tense. 'It's a plane,' said Jeannie, relieved. There it was again, a rushing, moaning sound. 'It isn't,' I answered knowledgeably, 'it's the wind.'

It was the sound of the scouts, the fingers of the wind, stretching ahead probing the hills and woods, the rocks and hedges, the old cottages, the lonely trees acting as sentinels of the land. They probe and jab, searching for flying leaves, decaying branches ready to fall, for flowers youthfully in bloom, for the green swath of the potato tops; and finding, they rush on searching for more, magnificently confident that the majesty of the gale which follows will crush and pound and obliterate. And when they have gone there is an instant of stillness to remind you of a quiet evening, the passing assurance of a safe world, and you wait; you wait and wonder if you were wrong and the wind is innocent; you listen, your mind peeling across the green meadows whose defences are impotent; then suddenly the slap of the face and the braying hounds of hell and the heaving mountain of maniacal power.

A Gull on the Roof

The east wind blew on Christmas Day, scything across the sea from the Lizard hidden in gloom. The black easterly. It slashed into our cliff, burning the meadows with the salt which came with it, tearing up the valley to the cottage, cutting into the cracks of window frames, rushing through the wood, screeching a message that bitter cold cold weather was upon us. And when Lama asked to be let out, and I opened the door and she gaily stepped outside, she suddenly stopped when her whiskers met the wind. Good gracious, no, she seemed to say to herself, *much* too cold; and immediately reversed into the cottage.

Lama

I find there is a certain comfort in the fury of a gale, a kind of antidote to the artificial standards of our civilisation. Here we are in this period of technical brilliance, a period in which scientists aim to conquer the natural forces of nature, in which academic doctrines lead us to believe that all will be well with our lives if we follow the rules they expound for marriage, for health, for social problems, a period in which standardisation has become the Nirvana, a period in which we are fooled

90

into thinking that there can be fair shares for all ... and along comes a gale. It lashes the land and boils the sea, turning ships into cockleshells, mocking man's conceit, reminding us as we listen to its roar that man-made theories do not control us, that nature remains supreme.

When the Winds Blow

That night, the night of the day when the strike had been settled, a ferocious gale blew up from the south. I lay in bed listening, though not worrying about it because we have long become accustomed to ferocious gales. It spat and roared and groaned around the cottage, and I lay marvelling at our good fortune that nature, not humans, was in a rage around us, that the wind thundered, not guns. At such moments one luxuriates in awareness of the real freedom. Nature is the king, not man. Nothing organised is attacking. No computer is smugly playing a trick. The gale blows, and is master.

Sun on the Lintel

Gales, then will always be our enemy but they are an enemy which attacks without guile; and it is easier to deal with a man who boasts his hate rather than with one who hides it. Muggy weather, warm wet sticky sea fog which covers the fields like a dirty stream, achieves its destruction by stealth.It creeps into the greenhouses sponging the tomato plants with botrytis and mildew, or blearing the freesias with tiny brown smudges making them useless for sale. Outside, it browns the tips of the anemone blooms, and sometimes it does this so slyly that the damage is revealed only after the flowers have been picked and have remained in their jars overnight.

But it is at daffodil time that muggy weather can gain its great victories. A gale can beat at a wall but on the other side you can rest in its shelter. Muggy weather gives no chance of such rest. It envelops the daffodils in a damp cocoon and brushes the petals, either in bud or in bloom, with the smear of its evil. There is no defence. You have to put up your hands in surrender.

A Gull on the Roof

Black clouds emptying their rain, were scurrying across the bay like upside-down mushrooms. At intervals the sun broke through, shining like a brilliant dagger on the sea. This was a sea that was glad of the turbulence to come, waves were slapping each other, leaving trails of foam in their wake, and watery pits; and above, yet so close that they seemed to be playing their own idea of Russian roulette, were the gulls. They dived at the waves, and swept through the spray; and settled, settled on the surging mass, bobbing spots defying the mountains which seemed at any moment to smother them. This was the beginning of the storm, the limbering up; and in an hour or so the gulls would have gone, gathered on sheltered rocks or inland fields, heads crouched in feathers, facing the wind, leaving the sea to rage.

Cottage on a Cliff

AT ONE WITH THE ANIMALS

Animals for me represent a form of anchor in my life; a reassurance, a symbol that in this world of envy, greed and humbug, innocence exists.

When the Winds Blow

It is easy to smile at those who gain stability from the love of an animal; but they are only being sincere. Trust is being given to trust, an antidote to the pace of life. They are rebelling against the standards of the herd, the superficial fashions currently in vogue. Instead of being greedy, deceptive, envious and slick, they are simply responding to affection. The secret heart receives its yearning.

Lama

Those who pander to their pets, whether they are dogs, cats, budgerigars or hamsters, are anathema to those who cannot relate to animals. Profound psychological reasons are said to be the cause of our behaviour: lack of love in childhood; lack of parenthood; lack of a direction in our lives. Yet all we want to do is give love without complication.

A Quiet Year

Love for an animal is no less than love for a human being. It is indeed more vulnerable. One can compose oneself by the assurance that a human being can evict disillusion by contact with his friends. But an animal yields trust with the abandon of a child and if it is betrayed, shoved here and there, treated as baggage or merchandise, bargained over like a slave of olden days, everyone except the cynic can understand the hurt in its eyes.

A Drake at the Door

I have found, over the years, that those who are tender about the feelings of animals, any animals, are those who are most likely to be sensitive to the feelings of human beings. In a personal, individual way.

When the Winds Blow

'Jeannie,' I said, 'we're never free. We pretend we are free. We tell people how wonderful it is to live in a beautiful place where the only traffic is the distant hum of a fishing vessel, where there are no neighbours to observe us, where there is no telephone to interrupt us—and yet we are not free at all. We are dominated by these two cats and a donkey.'

'And the gulls on the roof,' Jeannie added.

'Yes, the gulls on the roof,' I said.

Jeannie

There have been many times when we might have gone away for a night or two, only to be stopped by the thought: 'What will happen to the animals?' It was a vague, sometimes irritating, devotion to them; and yet if you live in isolation, no houses, no neighbours to be seen or heard, no constant reminders of the convulsions of conventional civilisation, it is easy for animals to dominate you. You revolve in a small world that is comfortable and reassuring. You are wanted, and you respond; and you receive rewards at many quite unexpected moments. It is a pleasant kind of domination.

The Way to Minack

I was unable to keep my resolution to be free of donkey domination for the same reason that I was unable to keep my resolution to be free of cat domination. Every day I was involved in them. Every day, despite their often independent moods, I was made aware that they were a part of our lives. They were not pets. They did not belong to that category of unfortunate animal or bird or exotic snake which are bought by people as if they were manufactured toys and then discarded. We were all at one. It is not a kind of attitude that some people can appreciate. Magic does not exist for them; and it is magic which brings an animal and a human being together in mutual understanding. The animal trusts; and the human being sees in the animal the qualities he would like to see in his fellow human beings.

Sun on the Lintel

All true animal lovers behave in the same way. Their love is so profound that they do not mind how foolish they may appear to cool-headed onlookers.

The Ambrose Rock

There are, of course, many who would call our attitude a sentimental absurdity. Why bother about the feelings of a cat? Why waste time on animal love when the human race can obliterate itself at the touch of a button; when twisted minds leave random bombs in crowded places; when schoolchildren threaten their teachers with flick knives; when there is a perpetual economic crisis? Animal love, in such circumstances, does seem absurd. It is an irrelevancy compared with the problems of the day. No wonder that pragmatic people condemn animal lovers. Life is too serious for such indulgence.

Unashamedly, however, Jeannie and I allow ourselves such indulgence. Animals offer stability in this unstable world. They do not deceive. They soothe jittery moods. They offer solace in times of trouble by the way they listen to you. They may not understand a word you say, but that doesn't matter, because it is a dumb sympathy that you ask of them and they give it; an extra-sensory understanding, which

101

is the more comforting since it is secret. You have no regrets afterwards for having disclosed too much.

Sun on the Lintel

An animal can represent a father confessor. Instead of talking to a person who is the dustbin of people's sins, real or imaginary, you unload your problems to a creature which mirrors innocence. You speak aloud and no one is there to hear what you say. You pour out your secret thoughts, and the burdens of doubt, guilt, worry, fear, begin to fade.

Monty's Leap

AT THE MERCY OF THE CAT

I developed a pose that after a while I made myself believe was genuine. I was allergic to cats. The proximity of one produced asthma. I felt dizzy. I behaved so strangely that any owner of a cat who was entertaining me was convinced that if I were not to prove a sickly embarrassment the cat had to be removed. I know there are some people who genuinely feel like this, but I was not one.

It was in this mood that I paid my first call on Jeannie's parents in their handsome house on the hill of St Albans. I sat down in the sitting-room and promptly Tim, Jeannie's cat, a huge blue Persian, jumped on my lap. Unthinkingly I played my customary part. I gave Tim a violent push and, in so doing, knocked over a small table upon which was my untouched cup of tea. From that moment I began to realise it was dangerous to appear to dislike cats.

For Jeannie is a cat lover, not only the slave of an individual, but an all-embracing cat lover.

A Cat in the Window

I had seen, for instance, a person sit rigid and uncomfortable in a chair because a cat had chosen his lap as the whim of its own particular comfort. I had noticed, and been vexed by her, the hostess who hastens away at the end of a meal with titbits for the cat which has stared balefully at her guests during the course of it. Cats, it seemed to me, aloofly hinted the power of hypnotism; and as if in an attempt to ward off this uncanniness, their owners pandered to them, anxiously trying to win approval for themselves by flattery, obedience, and a curious vocabulary of nonsensical phrases and noises. A cat lover, I had found, was at the mercy of the cat.

A Cat in the Window

Monty played his own part very well because from the beginning he made it plain he liked me. It was a dangerous moment of flattery when I realised this and I believe, had it not been for my entrenched posture of dislike for the species, I would have fallen for it without more ado. There was, however, a thick enough layer of prejudice inside me for me to hold out.

He would seek to play with me. I would be sitting at dinner and feel a soft cushion gently knocking my foot, and when I put down a hand to stop it my fingers were enclosed by small teeth. In the garden he would perform his most bewitching tricks in front of me, the clumsy chase of a butterfly, the pounce on an imaginary demon leaving a spreadeagled posterior to face me. And when at the end of the day we returned to the cottage, unlatched the door and went inside, it was strange how often he came to me instead of paying court to Jeannie. Did I perhaps impose an intuition upon him that my prejudice, once defeated, would leave a vacuum that he alone could fill? My prejudice has long ago disappeared, but I am still a one-cat man.

A Cat in the Window

It was another homecoming a few weeks later, an unexpected one, which finally witnessed my capitulation. I had spent the day in the cottage and was not thinking of Jeannie's return till the evening. I was in the top room alone when there was a noise at the door as if it were being kicked by a soft boot. I opened it and Monty came scampering in. He rushed to the sofa, jumped up, climbed on the back walking along it tail up, then down again to the floor and across to where I was standing, arching his back, rubbing his head against my leg and purring. All this in less than a minute, and performed with such élan that it made me wonder whether he was telling me in his particular fashion that I had been making an ass of myself. I bent down and stroked him, and he thereupon carried out a manoeuvre which he was often to do when he aimed to be especially endearing. He twisted his head as if he were going to fold up in a ball, collapsed on the floor and turned over, and lay with his back on the green carpet, paws in the air, displaying his silky maize underparts while a pair of bright yellow eyes hopefully awaited the pleasure the sight would give me. The reward he expected was a gentle stroke until he decided he had had one too many when there would be a savage mock attempt to bite my fingers.

But on this first occasion I was holding a pipe cleaner in my hand and I tickled him with that, which led to a game, which led half an hour later to his sitting on my desk, a large kidney shaped Regency desk with a top like a table, performing ridiculous antics with a pencil.

I was sitting there roaring with laughter when the door opened. In walked Jeannie.

A Cat in the Window

Although I have now been converted by the charms of the race, I still have no wish to have more than one cat in my home. I am, in fact, still a one-cat man.

I am, therefore, not a true cat lover. The true cat lover is ready to be obsequious towards any cat just in the hope of one purr in

108

reward. The true cat lover takes no notice of those angry outbursts, those abusive remarks, that a cat makes when he is unwillingly picked up. The true cat lover queerly approaches a cat with childish cooings, and is undaunted when the cat reacts with a baleful stare. The true cat lover enjoys blissful confidence that he has a profound understanding of cats, an unfailing way with them . . . and is unabashed when a cat spits at him. The true cat lover by nature fawns upon cats.

Cottage on a Cliff

Cats, I have now learnt since my cat-hater times, offer subtleties of pleasure that earn them forgiveness for their irritations. They have grace and style and a sweetness of movement, a detached elegance, and a marvellous devotion to those they choose to love. Cats are not for the coarse. I cannot vision a militant besotted by his rights having the time to appreciate a cat. A cat would be far too subtle for him. A cat, in my young days, was too subtle for me.

Sun on the Lintel

I have learnt as the Monty years, the Lama years, the Oliver years, the Ambrose and

Cherry years have gone by, that a cat can give you such true love that you begin to worry what would happen if you were run over by a bus. For I have learnt since my anti-cat time that a cat can love a person, exclusively, although the person has to earn that love by developing an uncanny sense of union with the cat concerned. Sad to think there will be those who read this who will say I am writing sentimental rubbish. Yet love, from whatever direction it may come, is the only true generator of happiness. So why throw scorn on it, whether it comes from a cat, a budgerigar, a dog, a hamster, a guinea pig, a donkey? The pursuit of materialism may provide us with the delights of high tech, but it can never provide us with that sudden glow which is love.

Jeannie

I have yet to meet a cat lover on holiday who is not worrying about the cat left at home.

When the Winds Blow

This is one of the sad aspects of the cat world. They have no road sense. It seems that cats have never, in their attitude towards moving vehicles, grown out of the horse and buggy age. Progress has stood still for the cat fraternity.

When the Winds Blow

An animal, as one grows older, plays the role of the teddy bear in childhood. He stirs those qualities which are best in one's character and is one's patient confessor in periods of distress. So it was with Monty. He was, for both Jeannie and myself, the repository of our secret thoughts.

A Gull on the Roof

Each of us had talked to him in that mood of abandon which is safe within friendship. Maybe it was only a cat's friendship, but secure never to be tarnished, easing problems because the aftermath of confession did not breed the fears of disclosure.

A Cat in the Window

He would glare at us from inside the dining-room window as we arrived home, the sweep of the headlights shining on his fierce face. 'We're in trouble again,' I would say as I put the key in the door. It was perfectly true that he had the knack of making us feel we had misbehaved, that two o'clock in the morning was a disgraceful hour to return home. We would switch on the light and hurry into the dining-room ready to gush a greeting, only to find he had not moved, that he was still staring out of the window pretending to be unaware of our arrival except for the sharp flicks of his tail.

A Cat in the Window

And when our guests arrived, a hundred or more packing the cottage, a cacophony of laughter and talk, cigarette smoke clouding the rooms, people sitting on the floor and the stairs, glasses everywhere, Jeannie and I rushing around with bottles and plates of cold food, Monty was as cool as a cucumber. He would stroll from room to room, pausing beside a guest when the praise was high, even deigning to jump on a lap, ignoring the cat haters, refusing with well-bred disgust any morsel dangled before him by some well-meaning admirer. He was unobtrusively sure of himself; and when the rackety day was over, when Jeannie and I had gone to bed feeling

112

too tired to sleep and we put out a hand and touched him at the bottom of the bed, we both felt safe. Safe, I mean, from the tensions among which we lived.

A Cat in the Window

Monty was an admirable conspirator. He remained perfectly still as she rushed him along the platform wrapped in a rug. Not a miaow. Not a growl. And nobody would ever have known that the night train had carried a cat, had Jeannie been able to curb her vociferous enthusiasm when she arrived at Penzance.

But she behaved as if the Crown Jewels were in her compartment. She was in such a high state of excitement when I met her that she did not notice the car attendant was directly behind me as she slid open the door to disclose her secret.

Monty's aplomb was superb. He stared at the man with regal indifference from the bunk. And as I recovered from my surprise and Jeannie muttered feeble excuses, all the car attendant found himself able to say was: 'Good heavens, what a beautiful cat!'

A Cat in the Window

In spring, Monty's thick coat began to moult and we used to give him a daily combing. He would lie on my lap as I traced the comb up and down his back, on his sides and up around the jowls of his neck. He loved it. He purred happily until I turned him over and began the same task on his underparts. There would now be silence except for a series of little grunts. He found it awkward to purr on his back.

And when it was all over I would collect the silky fur in my hand, go outside and throw it into the wind. It floated into the air soaring and billowing, eddying in the end to some thorn bush or tussock of grass or entangling itself in the sea pinks on the wall. It did not stay in any of these places for long. The fur was much sought after. Most nests around Minack were lined with it.

A Cat in the Window

All my life I have had a lilt in my heart when a black cat has crossed my path. It never appeared to me as an animal in that I said to myself: 'Look, there's a black cat!' It was just a shadow wishing me good luck, a dart which struck my superstitious Cornish nature. Time and again, at moments of unsureness, the fleeting sight of a black cat

114

in front of me had been the source of unreasonable comfort.

Lama

I glanced at Lama who was lying like a miniature Trafalgar lion on a yellow cushion in the porch. A black, silky, plush figure, utterly at peace with the world she lived in. A serene example of a contented cat who was sure of the safety of each day, of a regular, well filled plate, of immediate obedience to her whims. A cat who appeared to have no reason to expect that the comfortable progress of her life would ever be rudely disturbed.

Lama

Lama ... liked on a summer's morning to stroll towards Monty's Leap, taking her time, alert for any rustle in the grass, sniffing sweet scents, until she reached the stream where she leisurely partook of the water. The essence of this ritual was the way she could carry it out undisturbed. I would not have dared to interrupt her while the stroll was in progress; and I feel sure that if a stranger driving a car had seen her in the lane ahead of him, he would not just have stopped the car. He would have backed it out of sight. It was so perfectly obvious that she was communing with her soul, and had at all costs to be left alone.

A Cornish Summer

Cherry was proceeding to perform the particular gesture which cats seem to believe is irresistible. It is the turnover gesture, the gesture which results in the display of silky fur undercarriage, spasmodic wriggling on the back, and pretty poses involving paws resembling baby fists. This bewitching behaviour often produces cries of admiration even from neutral observers; and such applause, after a minute or two, signals a changing course of action upon the part of the cat. Having bewitched, the cat will return to his normal routine. He will collect himself, maybe have a token wash, then stalk away. He has displayed his power over the human race to his satisfaction.

The Cherry Tree

I was to learn . . . the art of stroking: the need to stroke a cat delicately, tracing a gentle finger down the back, a gentle finger criss-crossing the forehead, a gentle finger tickling under the ears, that as a result a cat's conventional purr erupts into a purr of falsetto proportions.

Jeannie

She began to purr. It was not one of those ordinary purrs which one must admit are two a penny in any normal cat-happy circumstances. It was a soar. A glorious anthem praising to the heavens that she was the favoured one to live alone with us inside the cottage at Minack.

Lama

He is a great purrer at night on our bed. I can be lying awake in the early hours, devising angry letters to send to those who may have vexed me by some action or lack of action (angry letters that I seldom write when morning comes) and my angry thoughts, as time goes by, are soothed by this wonderful sound of Ambrose's ceaseless purrs. He has always been a great purrer. When Oliver was alive he used to bash Ambrose sometimes with his paw, telling him to shut up.

A Quiet Year

I once again woke up at three o'clock ... A quiet night outside except for the hush noise of the sea, but inside on the bed, a roaring purr.

I have a digital clock on a chair beside my side of the bed, and after a few minutes I glanced at its flicking light and noted the time. It was five minutes past three. Ambrose was lying in elongated fashion across Jeannie. She was sound asleep. No knowledge of Ambrose's presence despite his weight. No knowledge of his purr.

I, on the other hand, lay there fantasising about situations past and future, the long-playing purr as background music ... Half an hour, three-quarters of an hour, an hour, an hour and a quarter, an hour and a half. Without a moment's rest Ambrose continued to purr.

I wanted to share the situation with Jeannie, and I nudged her, and she woke up.

'Don't move,' I said quickly, 'lie absolutely still. Listen.'

'What's all this about?' she murmured.

I saw her move her arm.

'Don't touch him!'

'Have you gone mad?'

'Ambrose is in the process of winning a world record.'

'No, really. You wake me up and are talking absolute nonsense.'

'Quiet. I'll explain in a moment.'

Ambrose had stirred; and the engine driving the purr was slowing down. Then it stopped, and there was silence. I looked at the digital clock. The lights flickered to twenty minutes to five.

'One hour forty minutes at least!'

'What does that mean?'

'It means that Ambrose without anyone stroking him or putting their hand on him has purred non-stop all that time. Couldn't that be a world record?'

'You really are silly,' said Jeannie, though I reckoned that it was a kind of silliness which she enjoyed. 'Isn't he silly, Ambrose?'

His reply was to stretch, walk to the bottom of the bed, jump from there to the window sill, and out into the night.

The Cherry Tree

I am inclined to believe that kneading is a more subtle expression of pleasure than a purr. A purr is a boisterous acclamation in comparison. The knead, that gentle in and out movement of paws and claws, is a private demonstration of serene ecstasy; and it is, I feel, the surest sign of all that a cat is content. The conventional knead requires, of course, a cushion, or something soft and inviting like the counterpane of a bed; but the happiest knead of all to watch is a cat lying with lazy abandon on its side or its back, nothing for it to clasp, no object being used as a victim, just kneading. You see then the wonderful secret thoughts finding their way to expression. A cat in a private heaven.

Lama

Ambrose followed me into the cottage out of the rain, a wet ginger sponge; and walked over to the space beneath my desk, and began to lick the wet away.

'Come over here,' I said, sitting down on the

sofa; 'let me dry you.'

He ignored me.

'Come on, Ambrose . . .'

He continued to lick.

'Come on . . .'

Jeannie appeared from the tiny kitchen.

'Won't you ever learn,' she said, 'that you can never persuade a cat to do anything it doesn't want to do?'

The Ambrose Rock

I recognised the fact that I was their prisoner; and I refrained from shifting my leg just a little bit in order to give it relief because I feared that in retaliation they might both jump off the bed and I did not want that. I preferred the purring chains. I preferred to accept the compliment that they had chosen me as the site for sleep rather than the hay in the barn, the sofa in the sitting-room, or the expanse of the spare bed. Thus I would lie there in the dark, yearning to bend my knees, stretch, turn to one side or the other, kick my legs in freedom; and foolishly choosing not to do so for fear of interrupting the purring pleasures of two cats . . .

Sun on the Lintel

121

This situation with two cats who did not love each other obviously upset Jeannie and me; and we had the tricky game of balancing our own love for them both. Ambrose as the senior, someone who had shared so many of our struggles, our failures and our successes, naturally required priority because he belonged over the years to Minack. Cherry, on the other hand, every day entering more deeply into our hearts, also deserved special attention. She adored being at Minack. We were the only people in her life to whom she could give her love. We were in a quandary. The old, old story when one loves two people.

'Tell you what we'll do,' said Jeannie one day.

'Yes?'

'It's night time when Cherry feels most vulnerable. There she is alone in the spare room while Ambrose is purring away on our bed.'

'Yes?'

'I therefore suggest that if one of us wakes up during the night and can't get to sleep again, we go to the spare room and settle in the bed for a while. Cherry will then feel fussed over.'

I looked at her in astonishment. She may have converted me into being a cat lover, but not to that extent.

'I think you're potty,' I said. 'Nothing, nothing will make me leave a warm bed to give company to a cat.'

Jeannie

I set off on my walk with the intention of taking the coastal path to Carn Barges, and then going inland to the top of the valley in which Lamorna lies. It is a pleasant, up and down walk through gorse-covered land with the gorse in places so high that, even in high summer, you are walking in the shade; and you pass through a copse where, in this particular year, I had heard the first chiffchaff in the second week of March, and you cross a little stream which tumbles speedily towards the sea, then onwards through bracken country and past bramble tendrils which try to sneak across the path so that I always take secateurs with me to cut them back. It is a walk that the donkeys love to take and, when I go on my own, I always feel a little guilty that I have left them behind.

I had, however, only just passed through the white gate which leads to the big field, or Fred's field as we call it, because he was born there one May morning beside a flat rock in the centre, when Oliver rushed past me, then came to a full stop and stared back at me.

'I'm going too far,' I said. 'You won't want to come where I am going.'

I went on down the path to the boundary wall and clambered over it and, as I did so, Oliver rushed past me again, then came to a stop in a damp patch of the path, around which wild mint grows.

'You won't like it,' I said. 'You'll start miaowing soon.'

I felt a mild irritation that I was about to be cheated of my peaceful walk. A sunny morning, no troubles on my mind, the air full of April scents and gulls' cries, and I was to be baulked by a cat.

Miaow.

'There you are, Oliver. I knew it.'

Miaow, miaow.

I had left him behind beside the wild mint.

Miaow!

It was a foghorn of a miaow. A miaow so demanding in its tone that I knew now that my happy walk was ruined. I had to surrender to him. I had to turn back. I had to walk where *he* wanted to walk.

Sun on the Lintel

Ten minutes later we reached Carn Barges, stayed there five minutes, then started to return for the breakfast of bacon and eggs we had planned. We had gone half-way along the path, reached a corner by a decaying elder copse, rounded it . . . And there was Ambrose. He had never been with us on the path before. Instinct had told him where we had gone, a form of love made him follow us; and the result for Jeannie was pleasure beyond the price of a diamond necklace from Cartier's.

The Cherry Tree

This year a triumph! Every tulip bulb burst into bloom and the garden was decorated with orange tulips, yellow ones, pink ones; and Jeannie, untouched by rational thoughts, decided that this triumph was due to the combined action of Ambrose and Cherry. They had decided to unite against the menace of tulip-eating mice. They would forget their personal differences. They would catch the mice before the damage was done.

She therefore decided they should have a party, a tulip celebration party. This is an age when we are so dominated by the need to have material-based good sense that feyness does not belong to the modern vocabulary. It is, in fact, a sign of eccentricity . . . The personal exploration of the mind is considered laughable when viewed from the confines of a city building; and there will also be those who may say that Jeannie was suffering from whimsical nonsense for giving a party to two cats who had saved the tulips. A seafood party; and it lasted all day.

Jeannie

Monty ... died the previous May and ... his shadow seemed always to be with us. And although, when one loses a loved one it is necessary to be practical and not to mope or to be indulgently sentimental, we yearned for the soft fur curled at the bottom of our bed at night, the sudden purrs, the wonderful comfort of his greetings on our returns, the splendour of his person—the colour of autumn bracken—poised ready to pounce on a mouse rustling in the grass.

He had been part of our lives for so long. He had been a friend in the sense that he had always been there to cope with our disappointments, ready to be picked up and hugged or to bring calm with a game or to soothe by sitting on my lap and being gently stroked. He had been an anchor in our life. He was only a cat, but he had shared the years; and thus he would always be part of us.

A Drake at the Door

His efforts to please me were touching and, if I went for a stroll, I would find him trotting behind me, a black shadow; and although such a gesture did, in fact, please me it also made me nostalgic. Lama used to walk with me in such a manner. Every path, every meadow had seen her with me in all my moods and, at the time, she had seemed to me to be immortal, as all those we love seem to be.

Sun on the Lintel

DONKEY DOMINATION

It is a handsome sight, two donkeys silhouetted against grey rocks and the sea.

A Cat Affair

I could not tell anyone that they performed any useful function, but it was easy to answer the other regular question: 'What do you have them for?' I explained they gave pleasure both to ourselves and to strangers, and that they were plainly happy in themselves. Every day they were becoming more affectionate and more trusting; and the responsibility of looking after them, which once I had feared, had turned instead into a reward. They enriched the tapestry of our life at Minack; and by touching us with their mystical quality of antiquity provided a reminder that in an age when the machine is king, all life is still sacred whether it has wings, or two legs, or four. There was another, more personal feature about them which perhaps only Jeannie and I could understand. They had become to us a symbol. They were the tangible reflection of the simple life which we were struggling to maintain in the face of the outside stresses which were trying to envelop us.

A Donkey in the Meadow

I fancy that Fred expected a joyous reunion, a pat on the back for being so original as to attack a newspaper, to startle an elderly lady, to cause consternation within a week of his arrival. He was mistaken. Penny was as angry as she was relieved at being united with Fred; and she chased him. She chased him with her nose, chastising his buttocks with her soft white nose as if for the moment she considered it a whip. She chased him round the yard and into the stable, and out again. She was so furious that she wanted to teach him a lesson he would never forget. Not on our behalf, but on hers.

Fred's reaction seemed to be a relish that he was loved on both sides of the barrier, a wonderful hint that if the imponderables went well, he would for ever and for ever have the most wonderful life imaginable. And so when Penny's fury had subsided, when Fred found himself once again a young donkey freed from his mother's strictures, he smiled, putting his ears back and shaking his head. I am certain he was saying that he enjoyed every minute of his escape, the fall didn't matter, life was fun and mistakes didn't count so long as there were years ahead in which to correct them. I feel sure that when he came rushing up to my hand which I held out to him, nuzzling it with his nose, he was telling me what a hilarious time lay ahead of us.

A Donkey in the Meadow

We opened the gate and took off the halters, and away went the donkeys. They behaved as if they were in a Calgary stampede. Back legs flying, heads down, turning in tight circles, then racing away up the Clover field, and around by the corner where we first saw Oliver, then along the top of the field and down towards us, and veering away when they saw us, as if they were revelling in a mad rush of happiness, but which might have been smothered by some action on our part. What Jeannie and I were watching was an example of natural freedom. We all want to obtain it, this freedom which is not created by laws, but by the joyousness of suddenly finding oneself freed from inhibitions and secret fears and the raging stresses of today. The donkeys were, at this moment, a manifestation of the freedom that the human race seeks. They were in a new world. There was nothing foreseeable at this moment which would ever spoil it. It was fresh. There would never be an end. This was an Everest moment for the donkeys.

The Ambrose Rock

My resolution to withstand domination by the donkeys was a fiasco, I am afraid, from the beginning.

I would slip out of the back door if they were in a position to see me coming out of the front, and slip out of the front door if they could see me coming out of the back ... and then set off on a walk of my own. Or, if they were in the stable field in front of the barn, thus barring my normal route to the cliff, I would go up the three steps to Lama's field, turn left past the corner where we have built a stone hedge topped with earth and full of flowers, and down another few steps into the *QE2* field. Then I would scurry or, more likely, Jeannie and I both would be scurrying along the top-side of the field until we reached the far end where we would slide down a steep bank into one of our top cliff meadows. We would then believe we were free.

Freedom would be brief. The donkeys' acute hearing would catch the sound of our hasty footsteps or, if they were placed in the right situation, they would catch a glimpse of us as we sneaked away; and thereupon they would set up a heartrending hullabaloo and the sound of it would make us feel sorry for them. After hesitation, and an urgent talk, we would retrace our steps, unlatch the gate, fasten on the halters, and start on our walk again ... except now there were four of us.

Sun on the Lintel

They had, of course, other more subtle forms of communication than their bellows. The snort was a joyous affair much used when they were released in a meadow they hadn't been in for a while; a scamper, a kicking of heels, a friendly dash at each other, heads down and snorts. It was a rich sound. A quick roll of bass drums. A proclamation that they were happy. At other times, I fear, the snort was only a tickle in the nose, grass seeds in a nostril; and then they would stand looking at us by a gate, or peering down at us from the field above the cottage, shaking their heads and snorting, as if they were blaming us for their temporary vexation.

A Donkey in the Meadow

An eloquent feature of the donkeys was their stare; and we never succeeded in growing accustomed to it. It was a weapon they used in morose moments of displeasure. There they would stand side by side in a meadow steadfastly watching us, exuding disapproval, condemning us for going about our business and not theirs.

The stare increased in its frequency after the summer and the visitors had disappeared; for Fred, by this time, expected attention like a precocious child film star who believes that adulation goes on for ever. He missed the applause, lumps of sugar, and posing for his picture. He was a Prince without courtiers. He was at a loss as to how to fill his day. So he would stare, and hope that we would fill the gap.

'Why can't we go to another meadow?'

'I'd like a walk.'

'Oh dear, what *is* there to do?'

And when finally we relented, yielding to the influence of the stare, and dropped whatever we were doing, and decided to entertain him, Fred would look knowingly at Penny.

'Here they come, Mum. We've done it.'

A Donkey in the Meadow

Her idea of a nibble was to grab the carrot from my hand. A huge mouth, then crunch, crunch, crunch. It was a succulent sound, the forerunner of many, many such crunches. Here was enjoyment of high degree, the luscious favourite dish of a gourmet, the wild abandon of someone who had forgotten good manners in the pursuit of exquisite flavours.

A Donkey in the Meadow

Penny is a sage lady. She appears to take life rather sleepily, but she is the first to notice a movement on the other side of the valley. Her ears will prick up, and she will stare in the direction of her interest. I have learnt to respect this watchdog manner, and I will look across in the same direction, and see the head of someone, walking like a pinpoint through the high bracken. She is also a donkey of deep thoughts. Fred, although he too has his moments of contemplation, is more of an extrovert, a donkey whose life has been undisturbed by change, and who has known love since the day he was born. But Penny, I feel, has misty memories of Connemara hills, and pulling carts in bog land, and drunken tinkers, and Fred's father, and small fields with low stone hedges, and a colleen or two who put their arms around her neck; and the day she left the place where she was born, and was forced into a truck, and taken to the docks and crowded with other donkeys into a ship, the sea journey, then another long journey by truck to Exeter where she was sold at an auction, and brought to Cornwall, and a year later to Minack. Penny, I believe, is one of those who finds life sad rather than funny.

A Cat Affair

We were impelled to remain loyal for a while to the memory of Penny. It was a form of the old fashioned custom of going into mourning. It is not a question of going around with a long face. It is just a question of having a pause between the old and the new. No haste to find a substitute for the one who has given you love for years. Wait, and let fate provide the answer.

The Winding Lane

Mingoose Merlin's background ... was impeccable. Jingle Bells, his mother, was a Show donkey; and his father, Romany of Hunters Brook, had appeared in the advertisement pages of the Donkey Breed Society as one of the most sought after stallions of his time. Mingoose Merlin, in fact, was a very favoured donkey. It was as if he had rich parents who had sent him to fashionable schools. He wasn't a hobbledehoy like Fred. Mingoose Merlin was *registered*. There, in the Donkey Breed Society's *Stud Book*, was written his aristocratic lineage.

When the Winds Blow

I looked down on the stable field and, as the light died, watched them.

Fred was silhouetted against the darkening sea at the far end of the field, head down, grazing. Twenty yards away, Merlin too had his head down, grazing. In the distance, across the Bay, the Lizard light flashed every few seconds.

When the Winds Blow

On Christmas Eve we took mince pies to the donkeys in the stable. A lighthearted gesture, a game for ourselves, an original diet for them.

'Donkeys! Donkeys!' Jeannie called into the darkness of the meadow, 'come into the stables. We've got something for you.' And after a minute or two, their shadows loomed, heralded by inquiring whimpers.

'Fred,' I said, 'you're about to have your first mince pie.'

Inside we lit a candle in an old-fashioned candlestick and put it on the window sill. The light flickered softly: it flickered on their white noses, their eager faces, their giant rabbit-like ears. They pushed their heads forward, nuzzling us in expectation.

'Patience, patience!' said Jeannie, holding the mince pies high in her hand, 'don't be in such a hurry!' And then with a quick movement she gave one to each of them.

As I stood there watching I began to feel the magic of the occasion. Our intention had been to have a joke, to enjoy the merry spirit of Christmas and now, unexpectedly, something else was taking place.

'Look at their crosses,' I said to Jeannie. The cross of Penny was black merging into black, but that of Fred was easy to see; the dark line tracing up the backbone beneath his fluffy brown coat until it reached his shoulders, then stopping abruptly when it met the two lines tracing down each foreleg. 'Here we are,' I went on, 'with two biblical creatures eating mince pies.'

'In a stable.'

'On Christmas Eve.'

There was the gentle sound as they shifted their feet on the cobblestones, and I was aware too of the musty scent of their coats. Ageless simplicity, laughed at, beaten, obstinately maintaining an individuality; here indeed was a moment when there was a communication

140

with the past. Struggle, self sacrifice, integrity, loyalty; how was it that the basic virtues, the proven talisman of man's true happiness, was being lost in the rush of material progress? Why was it that civilisation was allowing its soul to be destroyed by brain power and the vacuous desire it breeds? Why deify the automaton when selflessness has to be won? for a shimmering moment we felt the race halted. No contrived, second-hand emotion. We were not watching, we were part. As it always had been, so it was now.

A Donkey in the Meadow

I looked at their crosses, Merlin's merging into his shaggy brown coat, Susie's black-pencil sharp against her grey thin coat. In this age that clamors for a logical explanation for every mystery, it is pleasant that no one has developed a logical explanation for the cross of a donkey. Nobody has tried to knock the traditional interpretation that all donkeys were blessed with the cross because Jesus chose a donkey to ride into Jerusalem. How refreshing! Donkeys, brutally treated and despised, retain a therapeutic quality which affects everyone who comes into contact with them . . . There is no logical explanation because it is a spiritual quality which a donkey exudes, an indefinable awareness that a donkey is reflecting tragedy over the centuries, indomitable courage and the love which earned its cross in the beginning.

Monty's Leap

A GULL ON THE ROOF

We began to walk arm in arm up the fields towards the cottage. The silence hurt both of us. We had been consumed by the mission I had just fulfilled, and now we were left with thoughts that frightened us. We had not only lost our gamble, but were faced with retrieving its cost without anyone to help us. We had not bargained for failure when we left London, and its arrival, the sudden barefacedness of its arrival, brought unbearable depression.

And then, just as we gloomily reached the old stone stable and the slope which led up to the cottage, Jeannie suddenly said in a voice that sounded as if our problems had been solved: 'Look! There's a gull on the roof!'

The gull on the roof is called Hubert. He joined Monty as a witness of our endeavour and the pleasure that has come with it. He watched us fight back at Minack working for a year on our own. He saw us beginning to succeed then rushed by the elements into retreat, then forward again.

A Gull on the Roof

Hubert the gull, though it may sound absurd to say so, changed our lives at that moment. We were no longer despondent. We became determined to survive.

A Quiet Year

He was to us the symbol we needed. The sight of him reassured us in the sense that at this moment of material defeat, the wild had suddenly accepted us as it had accepted the generations who had toiled at Minack before us. The gull had watched and now was

146

prepared to trust. We had never attempted to lure him. We had never noticed him before. He was one of hundreds who flew every day in the sky above Minack, and he had chosen this moment of distress to adopt us. It was from that time that we felt we belonged to Minack, that we were no longer interlopers from the city imposing ourselves on the countryside, pretending in fact to be country people. We had passed the test. We were no longer looking on from the outside, armchair escapists who believe that dreams are real. We had been defeated, and there would be no soft way out for victory. We had joined the ghosts of Minack in the endless struggle against the seasons and, in doing so, we had embraced all the things they had seen and heard and done. We had become part of the ageless continuity of Minack; and the gull on the roof was its symbol.

A Drake at the Door

Sometimes he was in such a hurry to come to her that, if the wind was blowing, he made an error of judgement in his landing. He hated it when he made such a fool of himself and, after recovering he would sail into the sky like a flying god, majestic wings outstretched, with a symmetry of body that made our hearts beat in excitement. Here was the wild that linked the

147

centuries, noble, remote, free and yet gloriously tempting us to believe we shared something with him. Here was a thing wiser than man, luckier perhaps because he was not fooled by greed. It was content with the splendour of living. It embraced the sky and the sea and the rocks, struggled with the storms and gloried in hot summer days; it was a speck against blue and a crying, swerving, rebellious being that pointed black clouds, shining them by its white, uttering far distant calls, telling us who were ready to listen that the gale was coming again; the same gale, the same gull, the same human beings since the beginning of time.

A Drake at the Door

You can, of course, always win the attention of birds by throwing them crumbs, and you reap the pleasant reward of watching them; but it is when an individual bird enters the realm of companionship that the soul is surprised by a gossamer emotion of affection.

A Gull on the Roof

Boris also liked tomatoes. In fact he liked them so much that he appeared to behave as if he were a connoisseur of tomatoes. He was fussy about each one he selected, and he was not so co-operative as the blackbirds. He preferred to waddle along a row biting a piece out of one tomato then another as, in another sphere, an experienced wine taster sips importantly a range of wines.

A Cornish Summer

It is an uncanny sound the woodpecker's laugh, for it is gay yet sad; and I have listened to it sometimes and wondered fancifully whether it represents the laughter of someone who died when they were young. Such a thought is too romantic; but the truth remains that a woodpecker's laugh makes me remember sometimes those I have known.

A Cornish Summer

One afternoon, it was Thursday March 27th, we heard a chiff-chaff making its monotonous call, the first of the year, the wonder of its African journey transferred to Minack woods; and it gave us the cool pleasure of confidence in ourselves and our surroundings. The cry followed us: 'Chiff Chaff! Chiff Chaff!'—and the sound of its limited note, amid trees pinking with buds, moss brightening with growth on old rocks, primroses a secret ecstasy unless unexpectedly discovered, pools of ragged robin and bluebells ... the sound of its limited note derided the tyranny of the automaton age and the warped values that advance the putrid aims of the dodgers of truth, the cynical commentators of the passing scene, the purveyors of mass inertia. The dull two notes of the tiny bird trumpeted defiance of the fake and the slick, bringing to the shadows in the woods the expanse of its own achievement; until the sound gently entered the evening, and as night fell, hid among the trees.

A Gull on the Roof

The gannets dived a half-mile out, sometimes singly, sometimes by the score, plummeting from the sky, hitting the water with a spit of a bullet. The gulls fluttered low, watching as if enviously. Cormorants sped on their mysterious missions. Curlews called their wistful cries. And sometimes as we stood there the sea looked so meek that it seemed there never would be a storm again; and sometimes its rage was so terrible that we held each other and were scared.

A Drake at the Door

May ... and Minack had become a large, unseen housing estate. Wrens rushed in one direction, blackbirds in another, a feather in a beak or a moustache of dried grass. A woodpecker tapped at his circular hole in a tree, pigeons cooed, a thrush built a nest in the tractor shelter on a Saturday and a Sunday, then glared at me balefully on the Monday as I revved up the tractor engine, deserting the nest on Tuesday. Charlie the chaffinch preened himself on the bird table, shouting 'cheep, cheep', then away across the stable meadow to the undergrowth by the reservoir. Up on the chimney of solid granite, Philip the gull foolishly believed his mate would call it home, bringing tufts of grass, squawking. Bluetits, like flecks of summer sea, flitted in the wood; chiff-chaffs answered one another, Robert the robin begged for home-made bread, filled his beak, watched us warily, waiting for us to go out of sight. And all the while our pair of swallows were joyously flying around the cottage, skimming the donkey field, up around the chimney, black spots against white clouds, twittering, dashing in and out of the garage. May ... and the Minack unseen housing estate was full.

When the Winds Blow

The first swallow is one of the original

pleasures. Nature triumphing over man is always a pleasant act of reassurance that we have still a long, long way to go before computers rule the universe. Humans may be drilled into uniformity, but no one is going to control a bird who flies thousands of miles to Africa in the autumn, and back again in the spring to the same cave of a house, the same barn. So when I see the first swallow I rejoice because freedom still is with us.

A Cornish Summer

Swallows have a special meaning for me. Their flight, from South Africa and back, mirrors in my mind the existence of magic. I hold to magic like a lifebelt. Magic offers hope for the impossible.

The Cherry Tree

Such an achievement places human conceit in perspective. Our belief in reason, our worship of passing fashions, our endless desire to search for mirages as substitutes for true happiness, disappear into irrelevancy when one realises the majesty of a swallow's travels.

The Winding Lane

Nestlings were now in the nest in the barn, and the parents were skimming the stable meadow, soaring into the sky, snatching the invisible flies, then swooping down and darting through the doorway of the barn. No lavish spectacle devised by man could offer greater pleasure. A summer's day, green bracken covering the moorland across the valley, foxgloves pointing pink arms to the sky, the white plates of the elderberry flowers, carpets of buttercups in the donkey field with the donkeys lying outstretched among them.

A Cornish Summer

...lingwere saw in fish nest in the rock and
the parents were a training the stable members
coming into the sea ... signalling the invader
the ... then swooped down and darting through
the ... the ... in the rock. We have ... walked
devised by omnipotunt effort ... greater pleasure's
satisfaction ... in a green breath covering the
... and across the valley ... for some quantity
... ated to me. My ... The ophite pillars of the
marine ... the floor ... ranges of basalt organ pipe
in ... the ... date ... the overhanging
little ... cave into

A SENSE OF IMMORTALITY

I have never looked upon time as a hill, hiding the past on its other side. Time to me is a plain, so that if the circumstances are right, if the associations are in union the past can be seen like a fire; and the feelings repeated, recognised again after being forgotten, the old story of Citizen Kane remembering his beginning, of Marcel Proust's *Madeleine*, of all our minds when we are not controlled by doctrine. You touch the past as if it were the present. You meet yourself again as a ten-year-old at a moment of anguish or great joy, you are there again at first love; nothing has changed, you are as you always have been.

Lama

There is no house or eyesore in sight; and this freedom amid such untamed country provides a sense of immortality. As if here is a life that belongs to any century, that there is no harsh division in time, that the value of true happiness lies in the enduring qualities of nature. The wind blows as it did when the old crofter lived at Minack, so too the robin's song, and the flight of the curlew, and the woodpecker's knock on an elm. This sense of continuity may be unimportant in a world with the knowledge to reach the stars; but to us it provided the antidote to the life we had led. It was a positive reminder that generations had been able to find contentment without becoming slaves of the machine. Here around us were the ghosts of men and animals, long forgotten storms and hot summer days, gathered harvests and the hopes of spring. They were all one, and our future was part of them.

A Cat in the Window

'When did you come to Minack?'

I have a simple answer to this question, hating time as I do, believing too much emphasis is on age and time, in this flashing age of speed.

'Yesterday,' is my answer.

The Winding Lane

When did it happen? Three, five, ten summers ago? Incidents merge into each other leaving timeless intervals. I do not remember the summer when the drought dried up Monty's Leap, or the summer when I killed an adder outside our door, or the summer when a hoopoe paraded on the grass in front of the cottage, or the summer when I caught a conger eel in my lobster pot, and scared Jeannie when

158

I brought it to her in the kitchen. Important incidents at the time, they have faded into one summer; so too have the pleasant hours I have watched Lama, the little black cat, and Boris, the muscovy drake sitting incongruously side by side, the one purring, the other ready to raise his head feathers and hiss harmlessly the second he was disturbed; so too have the stares of Penny and Fred the donkeys, looking down at us from the field above our porch, demanding our attention.

When did it happen? I do not know which summer it was when we watched the fox cubs playing in the field on the other side of the shallow valley, fearing that some stranger would see them too, and disturb them. All soft scented days when woodpigeons clapped their wings in courtship, when a raven grunted overhead, when green woodpeckers called to each other in the wood, belong to one summer; all still nights when voices of fishermen, a mile or more out to sea, sounded so loud that they were like ghosts talking in the front garden. There are no dates in my memory.

A Cornish Summer

I become vague when I try to isolate the years. I would like to have them arrayed in my mind in neat compartments but I find instead they merge into each other, and incidents connect themselves by haphazard association rather than by dates. Thus the flower seasons here at Minack, each of which has a slow moving yet mounting dramatic entity of its own, become dissolved in my mind into all flower seasons. The hours I have crouched weeding anemones or picking violets, lugging baskets of daffodils to the packing shed, rushing the flower boxes in the morning to Penzance Station, these hours do not belong to one year but to all years. So also appear the storms that have battered Minack, and the lazy pleasure of hot summer days, the first scent of the may, the arrival of the chiff-chaffs, the wonder of an angry sea with a fishing boat fighting for home. I have grown older not by passing each incident as if it were a milestone, but by being absorbed by them.

A Cat in the Window

On I went along the path, across Fred's field, down to the little gate at the top of the cliff, down the steps, down through the pocket meadows, past the palm tree which I planted when my mother died, through the narrow gap between two hedges of blackthorn and into the bottom daffodil meadow of all, then down again to the point where the grass ended and the grey rocks began. Here was my journey's end. Here I stood with the grandeur of a Cornish sea just below me, watching it foaming the rocks where we lazed on summer days, watching the great waves mounting their assault, coming nearer and nearer, and growing, and the tops curving and sharpening so that for a split second the tops resembled a knife's edge before they thundered down on the rocks which halted them. This was a scene which belonged to immortality. I was seeing the same waves, hearing the same roar, wet with the same spray, nothing had changed throughout the centuries. This was the universe. This was the back-drop to all history, to all conflicts between nations or individuals, to impatient ambitions, to the passing fashions of each age, to the vanity of man. This was continuity which some ignore, some deride; and in which some find comfort. Man's conceit as he overpopulates, drowns the countryside in concrete, pollutes the sky and the rivers, will surely wither. One day he will learn the universe is master.

Cottage on a Cliff

There is no telephone at Minack, no noise of distant traffic, no sign of material progress in the boulder strewn, wild land which gently, then steeply falls to the sea of Mount's Bay. Here is a place which is poised in time. Here

161

the old rocks have observed through the centuries the vanity of man, the fitful moments of his power, ambitions lost and won, the fleeing days of living. The old chimney of the cottage prodding into the sky awaits another gale, another sunny day, another mist swirling in from the south, no different from the others it has faced for five hundred years. There it stands, a welcome and a farewell, sharing a landscape with the untamed, sharing the continuity of time. The years pass and the same moss is growing on the rocks, the same music of the waves plays at the bottom of the cliffs.

The Way to Minack

TO SEARCH OUR INWARD SELVES

My aim in life at this time was to rid myself of the strait-jacket standards my environment had brought me up to believe indestructible, and to find a way to be free of the restlessness inside me. I had no clue where this restlessness might lead me but, if I bottled it up, I knew I would never find happiness . . .

'All I want out of life,' I wrote in my diary that first evening at Joubert Studios, 'is to be able to say at the end of it that I have lived vividly.'

The Way to Minack

I have seldom been the person I wished to be, because the person I wished to be changed so quickly that I was unable to catch him. My Walter Mittys have been numerous.

Sometimes I have wished to be a steady, conventional type, playing safe. Sometimes I have wished to live a Bohemian life as varied as that of Augustus John. Sometimes I have wished to be a pianist, sometimes an England cricketer, sometimes an art collector. Sometimes I have wished to enjoy the deceptive applause of transient success, sometimes to run away from it and hide. Sometimes I have wished to be an intellectual, praised by the few, though unintelligible to the many. Sometimes I have wished to be gregarious among the sophisticated, sometimes to live the life of a hermit. Walter Mittys have filtered through my life, changing their roles with bewildering rapidity, providing me in their aftermath with many conclusions. Among them is a distaste for those who relish exercising power over their fellow human beings; another is that a fundamental contemporary need is to delve into one's own secret thoughts before becoming anaesthetised by the opinions of a crowd . . . and another is my everlasting gratitude to the Walter Mitty who led me to Minack.

Sun on the Lintel

'Strange, isn't it,' I said, 'how full of contradictions we are.'

'I don't think contradictions are unusual in people,' Jeannie replied. 'Everyone has them in one way or another. Only the computer wants to make people Mr and Mrs Average.'

The Winding Lane

One is born, I suppose, with a lack of self-confidence, for no reasoning can expel its mood. Some conduct their lives as if they have never had any doubt as to their abilities,

166

creating an aura around themselves which earns a respect that is undeserved; and there are, of course, those whose self-confidence *is* deserved, who sweep through life with élan, never doubting their talents, and these are the lucky ones. As for myself, born with a lack of self-confidence, I belong to the group who shout in the dark, who sometimes brashly pretend the fates are on their side or, in contrast, yield too easily to opposition . . . but the undercurrent is always the same. One is yearning for encouragement to banish the doubts.

When the Winds Blow

I envy placid people. I envy those who appear to lead normal lives, to have normal relationships, normal emotions. The complications of life which pursue the rest of us do not seem to affect them. They do not seem to suffer from imaginary fears or financial worries or contradictory secret thoughts. If you go into their homes, you find the rooms are tidy, the furnishings apparently new, fresh paint on the woodwork, and not a speck of dust to be seen. Their homes are as well organised as their minds. Everything is under control. There is never a reason for them to wake up in the early hours of the morning and worry.

I have always been a worrier. I have spent months of my life worrying in the early hours of the morning because I have never been able to take happiness for granted. Happiness, in my imagination, should be like a calm lake without a ripple upon it; and no prospect of a ripple. Unfortunately, although there have been many times that I have seen this calm lake, my imagination has also seen the ripples that might come . . .

I am, from time to time, pestered by other unnecessary worries. I have worried often that I have talked too much at a party, and said things which I did not really mean. I worry, of course, about world conditions, but that particular worry is universal. I worry about the greenhouses and their condition. I worry, in moments of hypochondria, about myself. I worry about the memories of long-ago meetings, which remain so fresh in my mind that I can vision the occasions and, in retrospect, be aware that the cause of their failure was my fault. I worry about anything in my small world, if I am in the mood. I am one of those people, therefore, who are labelled insecure by those who beam self-confidence.

The Ambrose Rock

Yet one must also face up to the moments of true depression; the moments of sadness, of personal inadequacy, of loneliness, of fear of the future, which sweep one into an undefinable despair. Such despair is so personal that outsiders have difficulty in understanding it, or realising its depth. Of course, there are the professionals who are waiting to give advice, but their chief role, their most useful role, can only be to listen. There are also drugs and alcohol to tempt a person into illusory relief, into believing that despair can be banished by superficial means. But the only way to free oneself from despair is, I am sure, by one's own efforts, and by remembering the old adage of counting one's blessings and comparing oneself with those so obviously in a worse situation.

The Ambrose Rock

We had in our hearts the exquisitely sweet relief of being freed from twentieth-century entanglements. The deceptive gloss, the gritty worship of false values, the dependence on the decisions of tin gods, all these we had escaped from; and we had the years ahead of us in which to dwell with the primitive and to discover whether within ourselves we could earn contentment.

One discovers in these circumstances that one's own shadow remains the enemy. During the honeymoon of the first years a magical impulse drives you forward, seducing you into believing that each set-back is a jest and each complication a momentary bad dream which has no reality in the life you are leading. It is easy to believe, at this time, that you have devised for yourself a way of life that for ever will be protected from the tendrils of computer civilisation. You delude yourself into believing that you have the same freedom as an aborigine of the South American jungle. Cut off from the do-gooders and the progress makers you feel able to find your own level of happiness. Unharnessed by man-created shibboleths and conventions you feel you at last have the opportunity to release the forces of your secret self.

A Donkey in the Meadow

Some enjoy the hallucination that if you tear up one part of your life and substitute another, congenial to your imagination, that you become immune to trouble. There is the gay, hopeful belief that if you can steel yourself to surrender the tedious, or tense, routine of life to which you have reluctantly become accustomed, problems inward and outward will dissolve. They do not. There is no such act as escapism. Wherever you go, whatever you do—emigrate, change jobs, find the dream cottage, pursue your true ambition—you have yourself as a companion; you have the same grim fight to earn a living. What you do gain, if you have the luck of Jeannie and me, is the chance to embrace an environment which you love, and which softens the blows when they come; for the expanse of sky helps to free us; so also the sense that the wild animals, the foxes, the badgers, have been going their mysterious ways for centuries; and the sea is as it always was. The reward, if you have the luck, is to become aware again that values have never changed, that true pleasure is as it has been since the beginning, that man is nobler than the bee. The aim to be free does not lie in association with the herd, for the herd has not the patience to probe. One has to delve into one's secret self. No one else can help. But if one lives in the environment of one's choice the task is made easier, the mind is more willing to explore.

Lama

It is the peace which you can find in your soul which counts; and the soul is your personal possession throughout your journey towards perfection.

Sun on the Lintel

Incidents like these filled our summer days, trivial moments of diversion, the minutiae of living. I would sit on the bridge, staring across the shallow valley, the sea to my right, listening to the sounds that belonged to these summer days ... pigeons cooing in the wood, a lark singing, a cuckoo in the distance, the flap of waves on rocks, a girl's voice calling in the cows, the chugging engine of a fishing boat, the donkeys' snorting. Yet unimportant in themselves these passing pleasures posed the question, the everlasting question of the twentieth century ... has anyone the right to slow down the tempo of his life in an attempt to come to terms with his inner self? Or should he surrender to the pressure of conventional living, accept the tribal customs, sacrifice truth in the pursuit of power, view life as if from an express train?

Most of us conform. We stifle the secret hopes we have for personal freedom but find we cannot kill them. They were with us before we were smoothed by habit; and though sometimes they seem to fade away as the years pass, we suddenly find ourselves faced with them again in the form of frustration. There they are, challenging our weak selves, demanding why we have betrayed them.

Expediency, we reply, we had to earn a living. We became involved in a career, and we were chained to its progress. Or we may be practical by explaining that we never had the capital, never could hope to accrue the capital, that would have made it possible for us to break the pattern of our lives. Or we may admit that we lazily allowed time to slip by. Or we may say that the chance for change never came our way, or perhaps we didn't have the wit to recognise it when it was there.

A Cornish Summer

Missed opportunities are what one regrets as one grows older; opportunities missed by a momentary lack of boldness, or a fear of hurting someone's feelings, or because, when the opportunity came, one was blind to its value.

The Ambrose Rock

How does one recognise luck when it comes in the form of opportunity? Material luck is obvious, but opportunity tends to be obscure. Hence there have been many times in my life when I have looked back on an opportunity missed, and wondered why I missed it. The opportunity is crystal clear years later, and yet at the time I fumbled, and lost it. Why? If you keep a diary it will help to explain, and I have always kept a diary from time to time but not regularly, because, as Virginia Woolf said, diaries should only be kept at intervals, otherwise the diary dominates the diarist. What, then, has my diary to tell me about lost opportunities?

I find, for instance, that my memory over-simplifies the moment when the opportunity was presented. At the distance of time, it appears bewildering that I did not seize it, there it was staring at me in the face, so what idiocy stopped me from taking it? But I read my diary, and find the answer, part of the answer at any rate.

It is that opportunities seem to present themselves when the mind is muddled by conflicting circumstances, intensely real at the time, but which fade into oblivion as the years pass. Thus the picture of the opportunity remains in the mind, but not its frame.

The Winding Lane

Hindsight judges a past situation intellectually because it has no means of recalling the emotion surrounding a past situation. Historians, for instance, in passing their judgement on a past event, are always at a disadvantage. They may have the facts, but they can never be aware of the emotions which created the facts. Similarly this applies to all of us when we reflect upon our past mistakes and missed opportunities. We may now condemn ourselves, but it was the mood, the now forgotten mood, that governed us at the time.

The Cherry Tree

I do not understand those who say never look back. By looking back the years are not wasted, and one can place the present in perspective. It is too easy to forget the facts, the incidents, the emotions that have built one's life, long-ago reasons which determine today's actions.

The Winding Lane

Nostalgia, and sentiment for that matter, are treated with disdain by some. I do not understand why. Since we live in an era of violence and vandalism, of mass destruction capability and dwindling energy supplies, and of unthinking viewing, I think those who can indulge in a little nostalgia and sentiment are lucky people. It means they have memories of pleasure to balance against the problems of today.

When the Winds Blow

It is not an easy age for peace of mind. The dull and unimaginative can achieve a version of it, as too those young enough who still believe that youth is everlasting, so too can those who are ruthlessly ambitious, so too the men and women who are so busy organising other people's lives that they forget to organise their own. All these have peace of mind of a kind. They do not suffer the pain of self questioning and remorse. They are certain that their standards are the right standards. They are normal.

But the rest of us, those of us who have to endure the doubts and personal complexities imposed by our imaginations, are labelled maladjusted and insecure, inferior beings in fact. It is curious how the phrase that he or she is 'insecure' has become a phrase that means a bad mark. As for myself I do not understand how any human being can feel secure in the modern sense of the word unless he is unbearably conceited. Philosophy, after all, is based on the premise that those who are trying to find the truth about themselves, have a sense of insecurity. Aristotle, Tagore, de Keyserling, any philosopher throughout the ages indeed, would have had no place in history if present values existed in their time. Contemplation was the motive power of their faith, periods of loneliness developed the truth of their wisdom. I wonder in what category an appointments bureau would place them if they were living today. Is there any doubt that they would be considered maladjusted and insecure?

One therefore has to try and find out about oneself against the wishes of convention. Convention needs to pump knowledge into you, not wisdom. Convention, in order to preserve what it represents, must act in the manner of a dictatorship, forcing each person to follow patterns of behaviour which, however distasteful to him, however ugly, results in the end with the declaration: 'I've got used to it.' The most repeated, the most despairing phrase of this period of the twentieth century.

When I was a schoolboy, at other times of my life too, I have sometimes felt the need to be accepted in some conventional circle whose members seemed to accept each other for granted. But such acceptance can never take place. I have felt all my life that members of a group, however worthy their intentions, are running away from themselves. I believe one has to learn to face oneself alone, to try to come to terms with all the opposites inside oneself. Groups, it seems to me, exist to blur their members from the truth, becoming mutual admiration societies except when jealousy begins to irritate. Groups, in my mind, have always mirrored escapism, not the individual who travels alone.

A Cornish Summer

For I had learnt that gregariousness hides you from yourself, and that if you want to know the real truth of living it is found in solitude. Then, if you are patient, a window opens upon a multitude of subtleties to which you were blind and deaf before.

Sun on the Lintel

Union leaders, the prophets of today, are unlikely to urge their members to look inside themselves, instead of inside their pay packets; and the rest of us in our hurrying lives, absorbed by financial self-survival, shy from the discipline which is necessary, preferring to find relaxation by letting our minds go blank and staring vacuously at the television screen, meekly surrendering the opportunities of getting to know ourselves. Instead, we drift with the herd, making ourselves believe that the hysteria of mass decisions, mass emotions, mass pleasures, provide the answer to our lives. Yet it does not require much effort of thought to realise that this is a false belief. Each of us was born with an ego, a soul, or whatever you like to call the sense of Being; each of us is unique, and each of us is a puzzle which we should try to unravel. Otherwise, we are like a man with the key to his own house, who refuses to unlock the door.

Sun on the Lintel

It was dark now, and the stars had come into their own, and I saw above me the bunched cluster of the Pleiades. I first consciously observed them when I lived on my South Sea island of Toopua; and they were directly above me then, as they were now at Minack. I hadn't changed much, I found myself thinking. I did not feel any older, any wiser. I still had self-doubt which would lead me into making a move which was against my interest. I still believed you were a lucky person if you could be happy on your own; and that such people were able to hear the whispers as well as the shouts. I still believed, therefore, that peace of mind could only come from within yourself; and that no outside agency would ever be able to provide it for you.

A Cornish Summer

It is the collection of trivial incidents that help to create the fabric of our lives. Without them our lives would be barren. Often we may be mesmerised by great events, great theories, great indignations, but frequently these are inspired by a kind of mass hysteria. In such situations, we do not belong to ourselves; we belong to a manipulated herd. We become insensitive to the trivial incidents, sad or happy, superficial or deep, which fill our lives with meaning.

The Ambrose Rock

The solitude seekers are a different breed from those who prefer to march the countryside in groups. Such groups choose such a way of embracing the countryside because of the company, the chatter, the pleasure of being organised. The solitude seekers, on the other hand, hate being organised, hate to chatter. They are sensitive people who find an inward strength by being alone, by being silent amongst nature; and it is such people who belong to Minack.

The Confusion Room

Of course there are moments of sadness, even of despair, but they are passing phases. No one who lives at Minack could have these moods for long. One doesn't need a counsellor to remove them, no need to lean on his or her shoulder for support. The support must come from within oneself, nurtured and blossomed by the beauty of creation within an untamed countryside.

The Confusion Room

Dreamers may walk our land; those, young or old, whose worries can be stilled by solitude amongst wild beauty; who can become refreshed by the sense of timelessness, and so free themselves for a while from the complexities of the struggle for personal survival . . .

I recognise the dreamers because they are the vulnerable ones. They come within the category of the insecure, those whom personnel managers describe as non-executive material. They are those who have romantic fantasies and expectations. They are those who will understand without you laboriously having to explain. They are those who, at some moment of their lives, may have failed to accept an opportunity which awaited them, or have been saddened by a hoped-for relationship which did not materialise. They are the sensitive. I am at ease with the dreamers. They are seekers of simplicity. They are at home amongst wild beauty because they find solitude a solace; a moment for peace of mind.

A moment, now and then, is all one can expect. Peace of mind can never be permanent. There is always, in the wings, failure, or anger, or frustration, or financial worry, jostling to destroy it. The peace of mind that I know comes from those moments when suddenly, exultantly, I become aware of the magic around me, aware of mysteries that man-made devices can never explain. I feel free of being a computer number. I am alone with myself. I am part of the magic.

The Ambrose Rock

NO RATIONAL EXPLANATION

I am inclined to churn over problems. I go on and on discussing a situation which other people might have dismissed in a minute. My behaviour sometimes vexes Jeannie. She is one of those who like to leap over a problem, making a decision by instinct. I too like to use my instinct, rely on it often, but also I like to ally it with a persistent, factual self-questioning. The habit comes from a distinguished member of M.I.5 with whom I once worked. 'Go round and round the facts of a case,' he had said to me, 'and suddenly you will find a chink in the mystery, and everything that puzzled you becomes clear.'

The Winding Lane

I marvel at those who neatly analyse themselves and the rest of us. The motion of living appears so simple after reading the views of the theory-boys on this or that. Summaries of their solutions possess no edge of doubt. A huge house of cards is made to look indestructible. There is no grey in any problem. Reason is king. And although I distrust such exponents of logic, there goes with my mood a certain admiration. I admire their confidence because facts, in my own experience, so often lie, mocking the conclusions based upon them. I am, therefore, unable to pigeon hole myself. I am a don't know. I wend a long way round to find a solution to any problem, and when in the end I come to a decision it is usually instinct that motivates it.

The Way to Minack

Ideas are inclined to float in timeless rotation when you live in the country. Unperturbed for the most part by man-made time-tables, you indulge yourself when considering a problem by never coming to a decision. Another spring, another summer, and you will find yourself contemplating the problem of the winter before; and so it goes on unless an incident produces an ultimatum.

The Way to Minack

We both find it wiser for us to follow our intuition than it is for us to follow reason. Reason, with all its pros and cons, its good sense and caution, makes us woolly minded and negative. Intuition, on the other hand, has led us again and again to behave irrationally,

186

providing us with the chance to achieve the impossible.

A Cornish Summer

I do not make wise decisions when I try to be logical. My arguments, on either side of the problem involved, cancel each other out with such effect that I am left hanging in mid-air; and I do nothing. I like, therefore, to act out of emotion. I find that what successes I have had in my life have been born out of flashes of insight, the seizure of an opportunity which would have died a sudden death had I stopped to reason. And I have usually found that a most inconsequential event promotes the opportunity I need.

A Drake at the Door

It has often seemed to me that many people, especially those who are leaders of a country, of a community, or of a cause, treat logic as a kind of lifebelt. They are desperately anxious to believe that they are masters of their own destinies, and that they can control the paths of these destinies by neat planning. Thus logic, backed up by elaborately documented facts and figures, provides the basis of any report on any subject you can name; and the imponderables are ignored because they are too mysterious to contemplate ... Sensible people are inclined to ignore the existence of those unseen, untouchable, extra-sensory forces which push us this way and that during the course of our lives; and this is because the Western world believes itself so civilised that to consider magic as a reality is beneath its dignity. Yet many of us know of incidents that have no rational explanation.

A Cat Affair

There are some people who desire a logical explanation for every mystery. Their tidy minds require reasons for anything they cannot immediately understand ...

The acceptance of magic, however, requires a special attitude, a fey attitude, an attitude which digital-minded people find difficult to understand. They have been trained to expect a logical answer to any problem and so they are impatient with those of us who believe in magic, who believe that much of our lives are governed by forces that have nothing to do with logic.

A Quiet Year

188

Yet, if one thinks about it, it is the magic of the unexplainable that will always rule our lives.

When the Winds Blow

ON THE SAME WAVELENGTH

If one views time as a plain, there is no age barrier between the young and the experienced. They share a flow of moments of sadness, exultation, enlightenment, shock, success, failure . . . for nothing changes as the baton is passed from one generation to the next.

The Evening Gull

I do not believe age determines whether or not you can be on the same wavelength as another. There is simply a meeting of minds of whatever age which instantly feel at ease, just as there are other times when people, hard as they may try to prevent it, find they resent each other, or are bored.

A Drake at the Door

I was going to experience the magic of friendship. No envy, a wish always to help and the blissful pleasure of being instinctively understood instead of laboriously having to explain.

When the Winds Blow

It happens like that sometimes. You meet someone for an instant and it seems you have known them forever. You meet someone else, and there is no meeting of minds whatsoever. When you meet someone, therefore, with whom you can enjoy 'the exquisite pleasure of being understood without laboriously having to explain', it is an occasion to relish.

The Cherry Tree

I was standing there thinking for no rational reason about friendship; and how delicate it is, first to gain it, then to nourish it. At first, when the promise of friendship seems to be there, you can so easily be shy of pursuing it for fear of being a bore. You know the possibility of this because you have suffered from such a pursuit yourself. Thus the alchemy which creates a friendship requires intuitive responses which respect no rational rule.

I was thinking also, on this particular morning, of the traps which threaten friendship. Never, for instance, take sides in a quarrel; and in particular a quarrel between husband and wife. You can be sure that any word of comfort to one or the other will be used as a weapon; and so, having comforted the one, you will have enraged the other.

I was thinking, too, about the disappearance

194

of friendship, that which was born of propinquity but filtered away when geography interfered, or time. Geography is the less dangerous. Geography, however many thousands of miles apart, will not destroy the memory of friendship. Time, on the other hand, can do so. Time, as people go on their way, divides them from what brought them together.

The Cherry Tree

I have often found that individuals who formed no part of my life have influenced me at crucial moments. I do not mean they have been aware that they have done so, nor that their influence has been on matters of much importance. But something they say or do reflects, it seems to me at the time, a part of me that I am searching for. I suddenly realise what it is I need.

A Drake at the Door

Somerset Maugham, certainly, had a special impact on my life, but it was the French writer Marcel Proust with his masterpiece *Remembrance of Things Past* who opened the windows of my mind. I was introduced to his writing when I was nineteen years old, when I

was full of inhibitions and puzzlement, and the sense of inadequacy. The windows opened and I found the distress I harboured did not belong to me alone. I found that his writing, describing his own journey of self-discovery, was the same journey that I wanted to follow. He gave me a motivation that excited me. I would try to lead my thinking life in the same way, trying to reveal my secret thoughts so that I could unravel the complications which beset me. Other writers were to help me on the journey, but it was Marcel Proust who fired the starting gun. He made me realise that the only writers I wanted to read were those who stirred my mind.

The Confusion Room

I was nineteen when I was advised to read *Swann's Way*, the first volume; and suddenly I discovered that my secret thoughts and doubts were not unique. from that moment I have seldom read a book without hoping that in the text there will be some message, some form of self-awakening, that will help to enlighten me in the manner of my living.

The Ambrose Rock

One of the great pleasures of life is to find someone who unties a knot in your mind, and so enables you to talk and feel without inhibitions. Even an animal can untie the knot.

The Cherry Tree

I love receiving letters because they unite the struggle of writing with the individual who understands what one is trying to convey. Here are two people who are on the same wavelength. A secret friendship between two people who have never met except through their minds; and who communicate in privacy. Such a privacy is the secret weapon of the book world.

Monty's Leap

If one writes books which reflect your own life, and so in some circumstances reflect the same kind of moods of other people, you make friends with those who otherwise would always be strangers. The connection is subtle. It is not that of someone wanting to embrace the aura of a pop star, or a movie star, or even the aura of a best-selling action novelist. It is a strangely intimate connection; and it may be between yourself and someone who is very young, or someone who has had experience of life.

The Cherry Tree

TRUE VALUES

We have had many contrasts in values during our lives, Jeannie and I. We both set out in the beginning, when we had left school, to achieve a full life. Both of us had a snobbish element in our characters because we both wanted, unknown to each other, to move into the apparently happy and glamorous world of the famous. Both of us, in our twenties, had this belief that when you were accepted in the fantasy world of gossip comment, and became the cause of such comment, that a kind of everlasting happiness resulted. The true tinsel of such happiness gradually dawned upon us; and that was the reason why we escaped when we were still young; and why, though returning to that sophisticated world from time to time, we can still find far greater spiritual enrichment in the very small pleasures which surround us.

The Cherry Tree

Jeannie and I belonged to the lucky ones who, having seen their personal horizon, had also reached it; and yet in doing so there was no possible reason for self satisfaction. It was true that contentment was always near us, but there was an edge to our life which stopped us from ever taking it for granted. What had become our strength was the base to which we could retreat. We had a home we loved. Around us was the ambience of permanency. We had roots. And so, when we became involved in sophisticated stresses which touched us with memories of other days, there was a moat behind which we could recharge. We then could observe quietly the enemy; envy, for instance, the most corroding of sins, the game of intrigue which fills so many people's lives, the use of the lie which in business is considered a justifiable weapon, the hurt that comes from insecurity, the greed which feeds on itself, the worship of headline power without quality to achieve it. We watched, and sometimes we were vexed, sometimes we were frightened. Across the moat we could see the reflection of the past.

A Donkey in the Meadow

Independence always poses this problem. People the world over dream of giving up their regular jobs, saying goodbye to managers with whom they disagree, becoming free of the relentless routine of travelling to the office or factory, or of enduring the stress of pressures from those around them. It is a perennial dream for many. Yet, if the step to gain independence is taken, another vicious stress may take its place.

Jeannie and I have experienced that stress in the sense that, for long periods of time, we had scarcely the money to pay for the postage stamps on our letters, and we lived on scrags of meat and the vegetables we grew. Yet never for a moment did we ever discuss giving up and returning to the London circle which we had left. Why? Jeannie's perpetual optimism was one reason. Another was that we shared a desire to find values in life other than those to which we had become accustomed. Surface values are fun to enjoy in spurts, but to live with them permanently leads one into a disquieting vacuum. Life runs away and there is nothing to show.

The values we were looking for were those which help to achieve peace of mind and, in our case, they were composed both of negative and positive values. The negative values from which we wished to be freed included the weariness of being with people who mocked sincerity, people who relished intrigue, people who smiled to your face while planning to cheat you, people who considered simplicity a fault, people who were immune to other people's feelings ... all ingredients of the rat race.

The positive values, on the other hand, which we set out to gain, are more difficult to define. One is in the position of a lover of Mozart, trying to explain the subtleties of a Mozart quartet. Many will be forever deaf to the subtleties. Many, and I was one, will slowly become aware of them just as I slowly became aware of the multitude of subtleties that have enriched our life at Minack.

When the Winds Blow

What is a basic value? Honesty is one, tolerance another, tolerance in the sense that you understand someone else's attitude though you may not agree with it. Loyalty is another basic value, and by that I mean loyalty to a belief that has stood the test of time but which is being challenged by a change of fashion. Ever-changing fashion is indeed always the challenger to basic values. Basic values can never be trendy, and so they are dull. They never come to life until a person becomes weary of deceit, endlessly repeated.

Jeannie

Our wish is to enjoy the life we have chosen, to share it with others, and to survive.

The Winding Lane

Innocence, in these rushing times, is becoming a lost virtue. Innocence is an ally to magic.

Innocence does not spoil wonder by analysing it. Innocence is the acceptance of the unexplained. It offers trust and respect, offers pride in work conscientiously carried out. Innocence enables you to believe that miracles are possible. Innocence means good manners. It is without guile, envy or hate. Innocence is a victim of the materialistic society.

When the Winds Blow

It is a sickness of this mid-twentieth century that the basic virtues are publicised as dull. The arbiters of this age, finding it profitable to destroy, decree from the heights that love and trust and loyalty are suspect qualities; and to sneer and be vicious, to attack anyone or any cause which possesses roots, to laugh at those who cannot defend themselves, are the aims to pursue. Their ideas permeate those who only look but do not think. Jokes and debating points, however unfair, are hailed as fine entertainment. Truth, by this means, becomes unfashionable, and its value is measured only by the extent it can be twisted. And yet nothing has changed since the beginning. Truth is the only weapon that can give the soul its freedom.

A Donkey in the Meadow

'What is it,' I said to Jeannie, my eyes on two gannets offshore, 'that we most value in our life here?'

The gannets dived, disappeared for a second or two, then reappeared, flapping in the water, gorging their fish. Then up they went majestically into the sky.

'The taste of freedom in its purest sense,' she replied.

I knew what she meant. Freedom was once governed in this country by common sense, just as behaviour was governed by conscience. Laws were then limited to guarding the framework of freedom and these laws were respected, just as the rules of behaviour were respected. Of course there were abuses, but the offenders had to risk the moral condemnation of their comrades, an intangible punishment which hurt. Today there is no such condemnation. We have become instead bemused by cynicism, and by the overwhelming mass of legislation which, although enacted in the name of freedom, is eroding it. Freedom is no longer synonymous with fair play for the conscientious, the loyal, those with pride in work well done, and the man who cherishes his chosen way of life. Instead, in this affluent age, freedom relishes the chip on the shoulder and the couldn't care less brigades, blackmail of the public by striking minorities, high wages without responsibility, obliteration of the corner shop and the small farm, and a creeping destruction of the values which aeons of time have proved to be the base upon which our inward happiness depends.

Thus when Jeannie said 'the taste of freedom in its purest sense', she was thinking as Emily Brontë was thinking when she roamed the moors above Haworth, mankind and all its chains banished from her mind; the glorious awareness that there are dimensions in living which wait to be discovered by those who are prepared to discard their man-made prejudices, open their eyes and ears, and have the patience to be quiet. Quietness is the secret. Quietness opens the door to sensitive pleasures. The noise lovers will never understand them, never know them. They may see, but they will not feel.

A Cat Affair

Freedom, in the old meaning of the word,

depended upon a give and take, a moral sense of what was right or wrong, for its preservation. Today, however, our civilisation has become so complicated, our values so warped, political pressure on government so great, that freedom has become an illusion for ordinary people. Freedom is now only a word repeated parrot fashion by our leaders as they rush from making one new law to making another. Freedom has become a mountain of regulations that few can understand.

The Winding Lane

The sense of liberty, however, is a deceptive emotion. No one is free today. We are watched by computers, blackmailed by minorities and ruled by envy. We have no spur, as our fathers had, to heighten standards, to explore the subtleties of life, to escape from coarseness. We are enclosed in a society which worships the supermarket, and noise, and treats the charm of solitude as a vice. The odd man out is a nuisance and must be stamped upon. We must all be lemmings. We must hide ourselves in groups, hide our individualities, hide our quest for self-fulfilment. We must learn to accept the notion that it is naughty to desire privacy. We must make ourselves believe that it is anti-social to have saved for years so that we can be ill in a private bed without strangers prying upon us, that such saving is a sin compared with spending the money at bingo. We must adjust ourselves to these attitudes, and be careful not to challenge them. If we challenge them, we will be given a label and our views will be ridiculed. Yet all we are doing is speaking for liberty and for those who have died, sacrificing their lives for liberty:

> 'Went the day well? We died and never knew
> But well or ill, freedom, we died for you.'

The killed did not just die for the lemmings. They died also for those of us who wish to live as individuals; and liberty is the power of the individual to follow his own way of life within a framework of commonsense laws and conventions. Now, however, the laws have become so extensive and complicated that only the few can understand them and so liberty, as our fathers knew it, is fading away. We can no longer follow our dreams. We need no longer reach for the stars because there will be no reward in reaching them. We must conform. We must pretend that we are all equal in brain power, talent, and the capacity for hard work. Like the fast ship in a wartime convoy, we must proceed at the pace of the slowest.

Sun on the Lintel

It seems that today's society is unaware that freedom's existence depends on the readiness to take risks. If risks are chained, freedom dies. Legislation is increasingly killing the freedom which men and women in two world wars died fighting to preserve. Freedom means people can behave foolishly, happily, imaginatively, and yet be ready to be punished if they break the fundamental rules of society. Freedom, however, demands a price. Freedom demands victims, just as those killed in the wars were victims. Freedom cannot exist if we are perpetually cosseted by new legislation aimed at protecting us from trivial dangers.

We are therefore living in a 'take care' age. When one ends up a letter, one writes 'take care'. When one says goodbye to someone, the two words 'take care' roll off one's tongue. The whole mood of this period of time is that of 'take care'. We are deluged with advice as to what to eat, what not to eat, what exercise to take, what stereotype behaviour we should follow, the list is endless ... all aimed to maintain our existence towards a Rest Home where we can look back on our lives, having obeyed the theories but, regrettably, missed out on the sybaritic pleasures. Thus freedom is being chivvied away not just by legislation but by media influence as well.

The Evening Gull

I leant against the gate, and I thought of the millions who had spent the day, as Thoreau put it, 'in dull desperation'; and there echoed Jeannie's voice in my mind: 'How lucky we are!' And I went on to think of the circumstances which had led us here, how a sense of destiny had driven us. No intellectual motivation, no conventional self-discipline. Just the happiness that was beckoning, doing what we wanted to do, not stifled by the phrase 'take care'. Disasters we had, and I have listed them in the Chronicles, but they never shook Jeannie or me from knowing that we were doing what we were meant to do. 'Take risks' was our watchword. Not 'take care'.

Monty's Leap

I leant against the gate, and I thought of the
millions he had spent the gay... The...
... a full desperation and new Some
remained alone in my mind, 'How long,' we
and—And I went on to think of the
friendships which had held us in..., how a
sense of destiny had driven us. We toiled that
much that... movement of self-discipline
into a happiness that was, believe me, doing
that we wanted to do, not stifled by the phrase
... and Dashed We had, and I have tried
the minute Dumas, but they in two world...

A HAPPY MARRIAGE

I pondered about the girl I wanted to find, a girl who would give me a steadiness against the restless, threatening background of my life, a girl who would love the same things as I did, who would effortlessly join me in the happiness of walking barefoot on Porth Beach, wandering along the cliffs undaunted by blustery outbursts of rain, a girl who would intuitively become a part of my life. Just a dream. I felt no girl could fulfil that dream. Meanwhile I was alone.

I returned to London, to the bombs and to the excitement of *Time Was Mine* being published, and the miracle took place. The day after publication I was in the Savoy with a friend, standing by the reception desk, when my friend, a newspaperman with an opportunist outlook said, 'Do you see that very pretty girl standing by the hall porter?'

'Yes,' I replied, having noticed her already.

'Well,' my friend said, 'you ought to meet her. Her name is Jean Nicol, and she is in charge of publicity for the Savoy Hotel Group. If you are nice to her she might put your book on the Savoy bookstall.'

Needless to say I *was* nice to her. I gave her a copy and a week later she said she had loved it, and flattered me by saying she couldn't put it down ... and she put it on the bookstall. I thanked her and asked her

215

out to dinner.

The Confusion Room

I remembered the first glance she gave me. An air raid was in progress, the windows of the River Room at the Savoy Hotel were boarded up to prevent bomb blast, Carroll Gibbons and his orchestra were playing 'These Foolish Things', uniforms clung together on the dance floor; and a few yards away from my table sat Jeannie, a naval officer at her side. The alertness of her glance is with me for ever.

I remembered the way she used to run across Richmond Green on a Sunday ... I would walk to meet her train but I was always late. Hence I would see her in the distance on Richmond Green, and she would be running towards me, a gazelle. It was a signal of her infectious enthusiasm for life.

My mother described her as a pocket Venus. She was five feet five inches tall, with dark hair to her shoulders, a twenty-two-inch waist, slim legs, a mischievous smile and a voice which captured me and many others. I would ask her to go on talking just to listen to her voice, and her voice on the telephone was bewitching ... She had a teasing way of using it, especially on the telephone. 'Hello, hello, hello,' she would

216

softly say when ringing me from Room 205, her Savoy office. Then adding: 'Me here.'

The Evening Gull

I remembered the moment when, as I toyed with roast duck and red wine sauce, garnished with grapes, I asked Jeannie for her full name; and she replied that it was Jean Everald Nicol. I remembered how I gasped, and how I said: 'Good heavens, you're the girl I'm going to marry!' and this because I had had my hand read on a Japanese boat sailing from Sydney to Hong Kong, and the palmist, an engineer, who read my hand had told me just that: 'She'll be darker and smaller than yourself, and her initials will be J.E.'

Monty's Leap

Then there was Auntie Mirrie's story of the Fairy Ring.

'We used to take Jean and Barbara for picnics in Welwyn Woods, and one day we were walking along chatting and laughing when Jeannie stopped dead, and whispered: "Hush! I see a Fairy Ring!"

'We all gazed. There was a tree and just in front of it ... a perfectly round circle of dark green grass. The other grass all around was the

217

palest possible green. We were all astounded. I had never seen one before. Jeannie said that the fairies will be dancing on it tonight; and we crept very quietly away.'

Jeannie had told me this story. She told me it when, one summer's day years ago near a cove called Penberth, we were exploring the crevices, long disused tiny meadows, gloriously aware of the fun of life, scrambling up rocks, resting on one jutting out to sea, saying in our minds that we were in love, and we were on holiday, and one day we would live on this Cornish coast for ever, thinking of mad hopes because we were free, because we were far, far away from sensible decisions, because we were intoxicated by the sense of antiquity which makes the passing fashions of mankind a laughing stock—there we were together when, suddenly, Jeannie said; 'Hush ... look, over there beneath that rock, is a Fairy Ring!'

Not a ring of dark green grass this time. A ring of daisies. 'The fairies will be dancing there tonight,' said Jeannie, just as she had said when she was a child.

Jeannie

It was before we had permanently settled at Minack. I had come down by car for a few days, and Jeannie was to join me by train at the weekend; and then we were going to drive back together.

Jeannie had various parties to go to that week, and at the final one she suddenly decided to bring Monty on her night journey to join me. It was during the period when an American magazine described her as 'the prettiest publicity girl in the world'.

A hired car took her back to Mortlake from the Savoy Hotel, then she searched for Monty, who was out in the garden. She found him, grabbed him, wrapped him in a rug, then proceeded in the car to Paddington Station, where she smuggled Monty into her sleeper.

I was on the platform of Penzance Station in the morning, and I saw her looking out of a carriage window beckoning me; and when I reached her, she led me to her compartment, and there was Monty on her bunk.

'The attendant didn't find him there till this morning!'

And she was laughing.

'Oh you are a darling, dangerous girl,' I said, hugging her.

Jeannie

I called the collection of tributes for the book *Went the Day Well*. Several distinguished writers of the time contributed, and there were some who were unknown, and for whom I 'ghosted' their story. It was during this period that Jeannie and I began to develop that sense of companionship, that chemical relationship, which is the essence of a love affair. We would, in our spare time, go off to see people who had known a special friend who had been killed. I found myself emotionally affected by the reactions of those we saw, but what I remember most clearly was the sensitivity of Jeannie. She was so natural in her sympathy. There was no need for her to be taught how to understand. Instinct guided her. She did not need rules to follow. She did not need training. I watched her, watched her integrity; and fell in love with her.

Monty's Leap

'Will you marry me?' It was seven o'clock in the Coal Hole, the pub in the Strand, and I had been waiting for her for an hour, and she had expected a row as she came up to the marble topped table where I was sitting.

'Yes,' she said quickly, glad to be let off.

The Way to Minack

Jeannie was delightfully volatile. It was part of her charm, part of the wild Celtic dash in her character which made some people say they

220

thought of a Brontë character when they thought of Jeannie, a girl of the Cornish moors in place of the Yorkshire moors; and there were others, as I did myself, who saw in Jeannie the passion of Scarlett O'Hara of *Gone With the Wind*.

Jeannie

Jeannie, on such occasions, is inclined to take command. I may suggest a line of action, but she will go her own way. One of my earliest memories of her as press officer was the assured manner with which she treated the British and American press at a Pilgrim's Dinner at the Savoy Hotel when Sir Winston Churchill was the speaker. She, though very young, handled these tough media people so easily, and yet her authority was not derived from a feminist kind of attitude. Her strength came from her femininity.

Her femininity, however, can madden me. It is beguiling, full of opposites, emotions swinging on a pendulum, suggesting the existence of well-kept secrets, provocative in the sense that I am sometimes aware that I am being led in a direction that I do not want to go. Femininity represents the wiles of women since the beginning of time, the reason for their power over men, and so it is difficult to understand why the strident feminist of today is so keen to surrender it.

A Quiet Year

Jeannie is the sort of person who will go silent when she is hiding her feelings; and although, in the process, she is apparently supporting me in whatever task I am pursuing, I am conscious of this silence. She is biding her time. She is reasoning that in due course, without causing any offence to me and without disclosing what is in her mind, she will gain her objective.

Lama

Jeannie's preoccupation with birds and animals was the result of her natural kindness. She wanted to like people but she had found that people sometimes let you down, animals never, and so she felt secure when she gave them her trust.

The Way to Minack

Jeannie's gift was the ability to adjust her approach to people, and do so with such naturalness. Thus she was at ease equally with the famous as she was with someone whose life

222

was obviously a struggle. Nor did age matter: children or the old received the same naturalness, and responded to it. Perhaps it was due to her humility, a humility born of her belief that all men and women are not born equal, that some are luckier than others, and she had been lucky.

Hence, at Minack she always gave a welcome to those who came down the winding lane. She realised that they might be nervous, and it was a pleasure for her to put them at their ease. Not even when she was interrupted in a task she was engaged upon did she ever give a hint that she was being inconvenienced. She wanted people to be happy, and kindness was the best way to achieve this. Many, many people have come down the winding lane, and have forever remained a friend of Jeannie.

Jeannie

Jeannie once imagined a joke method of measuring happiness. She invented in her mind an instrument called a happometer, designed on the same principle as a car milometer or a walker's pedometer, except that it was operated manually. Her idea was to measure each moment of happiness during the day by pressing a button on this happometer; a touch for a flash of happiness, a long touch for some out of the ordinary happiness. Thus a business tycoon might push long and hard at the button after a successful takeover bid, a politician perform the same after rousing an audience to hail a policy which gives him some personal kudos, and Jeannie would celebrate in the same fashion because, perhaps, she had been thrilled by the dying evening light on winter bracken, the sea beyond; or she had experienced delight in some small pleasure like an unsolicited purr from Lama.

Cottage on a Cliff

It was an unusual expression for Jeannie to use, and yet its simplicity mirrored her character. She was able to mix easily with people from any walk of life because success has never been a desire to satisfy vanity. She has achieved it unaffectedly. Yet there is an aspect of her which is significant: she is only at her best, in career terms, with top people. She understands their language. She is at a loss, however, when dealing with the unimaginative, and she becomes unsure of herself. But when she deals with top people she intuitively plays their game, to her advantage and theirs. It is as if she is playing on the Centre Court at Wimbledon.

A Quiet Year

'Derek,' said Jeannie, 'you say one thing, then act quite another. You are so full of opposites.'

'You too,' I replied.

Most of us are full of opposites. Jeannie, for instance, revelled in her time as publicity officer of the Savoy Hotel Group, where she was described by an American magazine as 'the prettiest publicity girl in the world', and yet she equally revelled in isolating herself in a Cornish cottage.

The Cherry Tree

The delight of her character was the way in which her zest relished our adventure in a manner so natural, so persuasive in its truth, that never at any time did she fail to enthuse even when I, crowding my mind with materialistic fears, blocked her enthusiasm with doubts.

A Gull on the Roof

She knew that if she so wished she could return to London and live again the sophistication she had surrendered. At any moment of doubt the glamour was beckoning. The gaiety was waiting. She could forget the water which had to be pumped from the well, the paraffin lamps, the endless cooking, the long hours of bunching, the cold wet days picking the flowers, the naked simplicity of her existence. She could leave all this behind. She could look back and call it a time of folly. She would not be the only one who wanted to escape, then found escapism too tough, and returned.

Yet she never did consider such an alternative. I never had to listen to her telling me how wonderful things once had been, or could be again. Nor did she put doubt into my mind that I might be demanding too much of her. Instead it was she who gave me the courage. I count myself tenacious but I do not enjoy taking risks. I foresee trouble before it arises and so I can argue myself out of taking bold action. Jeannie on the other hand, acting by instinct, will stride into a situation undeterred by reason; and once embroiled she does not retreat.

A Drake at the Door

At all times it was Jeannie's enthusiasm, her never-doubting confidence in our life together at Minack that kept me, so often, from financial despair. Jeannie was carefree about money. Her sister Barbara tells how, if she was given a pound when she was a child, she would cherish it. Jeannie, when given a pound, would quickly spend it. On the other hand when she was broke, when we both were broke, she never moaned. She was perpetually propelled by an optimism that convinced her all would soon be well.

Jeannie

For me, since the beginning, it has been her courage which has meant our survival. I have never seen her in despair. I can fall into depths of depression, and moan about troubles real or imaginary, but Jeannie, when I have been in one of these moods, has never given a hint of surrender. It is not a bossy kind of courage, it is a very subtle one. It has been sustained by her intense joy in small pleasures. One day in the spring she walked on her own around Oliver land; and when she returned she rushed out these words to me: 'It was so beautiful there this morning, and I only wanted to *feel* the beauty. I just wanted to *feel* the white sprays of the blackthorn, the first bluebells, the celandines and the first buttercups. I just wanted to *feel* the courting of the birds, the clap of pigeon wings, the scent of the gorse, the deep pink of the campion. I was part of all this beauty around me. I *felt* that I was, I didn't think it.'

The Cherry Tree

I had Jeannie as my sensitive best friend, and when I was depressed, feeling so low that I believed I would never be able to heave myself out of my mood, there was always Jeannie to caress me.

Jeannie

Jeannie always acted as a flint, both for me and those who knew her. Her interests were so wide, and the originality of her opinions sharpened our minds.

Jeannie

I have always felt when waiting for Jeannie, returning to Jeannie, a feeling of excitement. There has always been so much to talk about, personal, politics, literature, music, sport. Her interests were so wide that at one moment I might be arguing with her that I believed Hardy was a more profound poet than he was a novelist; next we might be sharing the view that the boring delivery tone of a BBC woman announcer made us turn off the news broadcast, next she might tell me of a visit to a one-time hairdresser during which he asked her who was her favourite composer, and she had said Puccini—'Madam,' said the hairdresser, 'how brave of you to admit it.' Or we might talk of sport, any sport, and the ideas we each had would be tossed between us like a tennis ball in a tennis match. Or there would be solemn moments about politics . . . This was the joy of being married to Jeannie. She was able to carry on a conversation about any subject, not with the dry analytical attitude of the academic mind, but with the warmth, gusto and common sense of in-born naturalness.

Jeannie

'We always have such fun, don't we?'
    'Always have had such fun,' I replied.

Jeannie

I thought, as I looked at her, how lucky I was to have married a girl who was as slim and pretty and feminine as when I first met her, as when the great Cochran had asked her to become one of his Young Ladies and she had refused because she thought it more fun to be Press Officer at the Savoy. Since then, since that moment when she sensed that a life dependent upon mixing with the famous and the ambitious could be over-prolonged, becoming a frivolous vacuum, she had been a peasant, working with her hands in the soil, coping with the primitive life, and never questioning the wisdom of the change. She had learnt the true values; and so she was unaffected by the fact that her book *Meet Me at the Savoy* turned her into a legend, and that her novels *Hotel Regina* and *Home is the Hotel* had been mentioned in the same category as Arnold Bennett's *Imperial Palace* and Vicki Baum's *Grand Hotel*; and that her paintings and drawings of Minack had been sold all over the world. Her femininity and child-like impetuosity remained, and her contentment.

Sun on the Lintel

A happy marriage, a fundamentally happy marriage, is based on a string of unorganised emotions which cannot be defined in logical language. Jeannie and I had rows, but they were only the eruption of bad temper. They never simmered . . .

We were in tune, for instance, as to what we wanted out of life. We both wanted success when we were young, and we both achieved it. I as a columnist and as a result of my first three books, Jeannie as the legendary publicity girl of the Savoy Hotel Group. We had each begun our lives in London without knowing a soul, yet proceeded to become close friends with those who had been our heroes and heroines. But once we had experienced this success, we both came to the conclusion that that we had no wish indefinitely to maintain it.

We wanted to change direction when we still had time to begin a new life. We wanted to be free. We wanted to avoid being slaves of big corporations. Thus we came to Minack; and from the moment we made our home on this wild Cornish coast there was not an instant when we wanted to leave it.

The Confusion Room

If you live with someone and there are no office hours to separate you, no other life to lead, one has to be on guard against the groove. There you are, fulfilling the halcyon dream, two people who have come together, the end achieved which you hoped for at the beginning, daylight hours shared, boss to each other; and yet unless you remain separate, each a subtle stranger to the other, dullness sets in. There must be no quenching of conflict. Each sometimes must be misunderstood. Propinquity must not be allowed victory because conventional happiness has been won.

The Way to Minack

'Aren't we lucky,' said Jeannie, 'to have each other?'

'Aren't we lucky?' was a phrase used often by Jeannie. It was a mirror of her personality. She never took happiness for granted.

Jeannie

How many, I thought, have such luck?

Yet our happiness had not been built on a placid life. We had our rows, our anxieties. We were not always virtuous in the conventional sense. We had learnt, for instance, that frustration threatens happiness. Satisfy frustration, therefore, and happiness endures. We lived, therefore, dangerously and did so because deep, deep down we knew that we belonged totally to each other, and that we were each other's harbour. We had learnt, too, that unsatisfied frustration can turn small incidents into major ones.

The Evening Gull

We lived dangerously in the sense that we believed the secret of a prolonged, happy marriage is to live subtly free. I remember saying to Jeannie that I was not going to display tantrums if she wished to go out with a man, and I remember her reply which made me laugh. We had been married a week. She used a cricket phrase. 'Oh,' she said, 'I like that. I like the thought that I can have a change of bowling!'

Jeannie and I never found that casual friendships caused harm, but we both realised we were lucky. We shared a base, and we were always to share one. I likened it to a harbour: we were free to sail out of the harbour, knowing that the security of it awaited our return.

The Confusion Room

'I've learnt something about you today,' said Jeannie, 'that I didn't know before.'

'The secret of a happy marriage—the unexpected keeps it alive,' I replied.

The Cherry Tree

All my years with Jeannie have been an adventure; the frivolous, glamorous times of London ... or the first night at Minack when we slept on a mattress on the floor while the rain dripped through a hole in the roof. The companionship I have had with her has had its warmth through the unexpected. I am unable to take her for granted. She is elusive, provocative, feminine, always ready to make a sacrifice, showing faith in reality by not running away from it, yet always on the verge of chasing wild, imaginative Celtic dreams. No dullness with Jeannie.

A Cornish Summer

My life with Jeannie has never been dull. We have been happy in each other's company because we have not followed the conventional rules. A close relationship is the basis of a happy marriage, but a rigid one is not. A rigid relationship is usually the cause of marriage disaster, for it results in frustration and this, in turn, produces accusations of over-possessiveness. If two people have found they share the same attitude to life, an attitude which is intuitive, then it is foolish to be over-possessive. It is part of the fun of a happy marriage to pretend you are both independent, but that there is always a harbour to return to.

The Ambrose Rock

'Sometimes I wonder, Jeannie,' I said, 'how we have done what we have done in our lives.

Neither of us has a brain which is equipped to delve into detail.'

'I think we have common sense,' she said, 'and I think we both have intuition.'

The Ambrose Rock

We were together in these matters, as we had been in the beginning. Our relationship had never been determined by conventional standards. We had always believed in living dangerously, undeterred by passing fancies, because we both knew the base was true. Marriage can become dull if the rules are obeyed. Marriage, a successful marriage, must never be allowed to quell the illusion of freedom. Marriage must be a love affair.

The Winding Lane

She was wearing her red coat, red, her lucky colour, on that day in September when she left for the hospital. It was a morning of thick mist, and while she was packing, I hurried, hidden in the mist, to the Ambrose Rock. I knew there were small pebbles in a crevice, and I collected one, and brought it back to Jeannie.

'For you to take with you,' I said, knowing

she believed the Ambrose Rock was a magic rock.

When it was time to leave she first went up to the bridge, and blew kisses towards Carn Barges which she couldn't see because of the mist; and then to the Lama field behind where she was standing, and to the cottage. There was almost a gaiety about her, and she called out: 'I love Minack! I love Minack!'

Jeannie

25 January

One of the most idyllic days of our lives. We were *so* close. We went to the Honeysuckle Meadow. It was eleven in the morning, the sun was shining, soft air full of sea scents, and a bee came flying around as we sat on the rickety seat, deceived into believing it was a spring morning.

'Oh, I'm so happy here,' Jeannie said.

Ambrose had come with us, and was sitting on the seat beside her, so I took a photograph of them both with my new toy, the polaroid.

'I suppose,' she went on, 'that we both have achieved all that we wanted to achieve when we were in our teens, dreaming about the future.'

'Not many can say that.'

'Neither of us have ever been greedy. I

236

mean we have been thrilled by any success we have achieved, but our ultimate aim has always been to try to have peace of mind. If one is greedy, one never can have peace of mind.'

Jeannie

I was suffering from a sense of unreality. Could it be true? Could it possibly be true that my life with Jeannie was now only a dream? I now belonged to the great concourse who have experienced the ending of love.

The Evening Gull

Grief fades, they say, but I do not want it to fade. I do not want to think of waking up one morning and going through the day without remembering Jeannie. I always want to feel she is with me. I always want to feel that her spirit pervades Minack, and that her smile is hovering in the air.

The Evening Gull

I do not think she believed she was dying.

There was, therefore, no organised farewell, and this I find comforting. It makes dying an ordinary, everyday affair, making it so natural an event, that the shock of it is softened. I mean that in some curious way one feels that it has never happened, and that life will continue, although the body will be absent; and because there was no final farewell, I feel that Jeannie has never left me.

The Evening Gull

I have found, however, reasons for rejoicing that I am the one who was left. I rejoice because I could care for Jeannie until she died. I rejoice because I was the one who had to face up to the details, the awesome details, that followed. I rejoice because I was the one who had to face up to the hiatus of being alone. Jeannie was spared all this, spared the burden of readjustment. I feel I am repaying her love over the years.

The Confusion Room

The survivor can gain inner strength by being able to prove the depth of his love. He faces all the readjustments, copes with the sorrow and
238

the loneliness, eased by the knowledge he has spared the one he loved the agony.

The Evening Gull

My personal view of my future has always been a simple one. It is this. The only fear about death is the fear of what happens to the loved one, or the animals, who are left. 'Who will look after them?' is the worry.

Thus, if you die alone, without this fear, you die free.

The Evening Gull

UNSPOILT FOR POSTERITY

The lintel was ... massive enough to be there fifty, a hundred, two hundred years into the future; and I wonder whose eyes and what kind of people will be looking at it then.

I have ideas as to what kind of people I would like them to be. I would like people to live here who do not adopt a façade, acting as if effect is of greater value than reality. I would like them to believe that life is a mystery and not an organisation ruled by human beings. I would not like them to be people who are envious of others, who spend more time looking for faults than appreciating virtues; and I would not like them to be social butterflies who prefer chatter to silence. I would like them to be aware of the past, relish the present, and be not too concerned about the future. I would not like them to have orderly minds, because orderly minds would object to the inconvenience of living far from the routine of a housing centre. I would like them to be dreamers, irrational people who are not enslaved by conventional attitudes and contemporary fads; and, as a result, they would be so immersed in the magic of Minack that they would find themselves believing that they had lived here before. They would be stayers, therefore. They would not run away

243

when winter came. They would belong.

Sun on the Lintel

It is an evergreen privilege to share Minack with those who, though living far, far away, have become involved, and are prepared to come nervously down the winding lane, and across Monty's Leap.

Monty's Leap

'I was asking what you would do if I were run over by a bus.'
'You know very well what I would do. I would stay here. I will stay here for ever and for ever, I will be here when I die, my spirit will be everywhere. I will love all those who live here and love Minack, but if any philistine misuses Minack, I'll turn into a witch and haunt them!'

Jeannie

We cherish Minack because, in spirit, we feel we own it, will always own it, long after we have gone.

When the Winds Blow

It was this Oliver land, twenty acres of it stretching to Carn Barges and the ancient, rough undergrowth falling down to the sea, that Jeannie and I were able to buy; and to save it from exploitation of one kind or another. It was this land for which Jeannie had a passion. So fierce was this passion that sometimes she made me believe she was instinctively convinced it was her destiny to preserve it for posterity ... preserve it, not for aggro ramblers, but for those who seek solitude, for the insects, the badgers, the foxes, the birds which travel from afar to make their nests in brambles and undergrowth; and for the wild flowers and grasses which flourish untidily in glorious, unmanaged beauty.

The Evening Gull

She had the love for Minack that Scarlett O'Hara had for Tara. She believed that Minack, and this wild section of the Cornish coast, was a symbol of tranquillity, unsullied by tawdry opportunism, unsullied by material exploitation, unsullied by the deviousness of the human race.

The Confusion Room

It was a rich moment of our lives when on our first day of ownership we bent down and touched the earth, pledging that whatever happened to either of us this land would forever belong to untamed Cornwall. It was then that the idea of the Minack Chronicles Trust was born.

The Confusion Room

Oliver land, as far as we were concerned, was sacrosanct. We wanted to ensure that it remained as it is today forever and forever, a haven for badgers and foxes, for whitethroats who travel in the spring from Africa to nest in the bramble and bracken covered ancient hedges. Oliver land is a place for snipe and woodcock to hide in the winter, for pheasants to be free from a gun, for bluebells to scent the air in profusion, wild violets to cover the banks and the white stitchwort to herald the early summer. A place for the sensitive to wander in. A place barred to the aggressive ones, those who are always harping on their imaginary rights rather than relaxing their minds in the untamed beauty around them. The sensitive are always welcome to Oliver land, the aggressive never.

The Cherry Tree

I had come home to continue with one aim: to preserve Minack unspoilt for posterity, preserve it for those who seek solitude, for those who wish to unwind, viewing the jagged world and their own lives in perspective. Not just for those who come here, but a place for faraway people to travel to in their minds.

Money's Leap

The rain served as a curtain around me, holding memories of Jeannie, keeping at bay imaginary anxieties, remembering happy moments, exciting me with optimism for the future ... and always protecting the escape route for those ... who believe they can find a peace for themselves at Minack, in mind or in reality.

The Confusion Room

The LARGE PRINT HOME LIBRARY

If you have enjoyed this Large Print book and would like to build up your own collection of Large Print books and have them delivered direct to your door, please contact The Large Print Home Library.

The Large Print Home Library offers you a full service:

☆ **Created to support your local library**

☆ **Delivery direct to your door**

☆ **Easy-to-read type & attractively bound**

☆ **The very best authors**

☆ **Special low prices**

For further details either call Customer Services on 01225 443400 or write to us at:

The Large Print Home Library
FREEPOST (BA 1686/1)
Bath BA2 3SZ